TRAINING ACROSS MULTIPLE LOCATIONS

A PUBLICATION IN THE BERRETT-KOEHLER ORGANIZATIONAL PERFORMANCE SERIES

Richard A. Swanson & Barbara L. Swanson
SERIES EDITORS

Other books in this series include

Analysis for Improving Performance
Corporate Creativity
Effective Training Strategies
Human Resource Development Research Handbook
Structured On-the-Job Training
Results

TRAINING ACROSS MULTIPLE LOCATIONS

DEVELOPING A SYSTEM THAT WORKS

Stephen F. Krempl

R. Wayne Pace

BERRETT-KOEHLER PUBLISHERS, INC.
San Francisco

Berrett-Koehler Publishers, Inc.
450 Sansome Street, Suite 1200
San Francisco, CA 94111-3320
Tel: (415) 288-0260
Fax: (415) 362-2512
www.bkconnection.com

ORDERING INFORMATION
Quantity sales. Special discounts are available on quantity purchases by
corporations, associations, and others. For details, contact the "Special
Sales Department" at the Berrett-Koehler address above.

Individual sales. Berrett-Koehler publications are available through most
bookstores. They can also be ordered direct from Berrett-Koehler: Tel:
(800) 929-2929; Fax: (802) 864-7626; www.bkconnection.com

Orders for college textbook/course adoption use. Please contact Berrett-
Koehler:Tel: (800) 929-2929; Fax: (802) 864-7626.

Orders by U.S. trade bookstores and wholesalers. Please contact
Publishers Group West, 1700 Fourth Street, Berkeley, CA 94710. Tel: (510)
528-1444; Fax (510) 528-3444.

Production Management: Michael Bass & Associates

 Printed in the United States of America
Printed on acid-free and recycled paper that is composed of 85%
recovered fiber, including 15% post consumer waste.

Library of Congress Cataloging-in-Publication Data
Krempl, Stephen, 1959-
    Training across multiple locations : developing a system that works /
Stephen Krempl, R. Wayne Pace.
        p. cm.
    ISBN 1-57675-157-0
    1. Employees—Training of 2. Branches (Business enterprises) I. Pace,
R. Wayne. II. Title.
    HF5549.5.T7 K6954 2000
    658.3'12404—dc21   00-012325

First Edition
05   04   03   02   01   10 9 8 7 6 5 4 3 2 1

This book is dedicated to all the training professionals who face the many challenges in managing training organizations across multiple locations.

CONTENTS

Preface   ix

CHAPTER **1**
The Nature of Multiple-Location T&D Systems   1

CHAPTER **2**
A Model for Creating a Multiple-Location T&D System   17

CHAPTER **3**
Using Business Functions as a Frame of Reference   57

CHAPTER **4**
The Role of Technology in the System   74

CHAPTER **5**
Managing Multiple-Location Systems through
Regional Centers   107

CHAPTER **6**
How to Assess Performance   146

CHAPTER **7**
How to Ensure Survival   165

CHAPTER **8**
How to Build Organizational Capability   191

CHAPTER **9**
A Call to Action   211

Appendix: Communication Climate Inventory   217

References   221

Index   227

About the Authors   236

PREFACE

When a manager could walk down the hallway and see all her employees, the issues of knowledge transfer and training were fairly simple. Trainers and employees shared a common culture and worldviews; they met under one roof for training. As the training concluded, they returned to offices in the same area so that they could continue to learn from one another. But this is a new millennium. Transportation and telecommunication advances have transformed corporate life. Many corporations are going global. Offices, retail stores, and restaurants that are part of the same organization may be located in a dozen other countries. The workforce is dispersed. Languages and cultures differ. Control shifts constantly between headquarters and local offices.

For the training and development (T&D) community, this globalization brings both challenge and reward. The challenge is to distribute knowledge and implement training across cultural, language, and geographic boundaries, to balance corporate standardization with local customization. The reward lies in being part of —or even presiding over—a T&D function that is unified in vision, values, and practices and that strives to spread the corporate "mantra" while retaining the flexibility to incorporate local ideas from multiple locations.

The worldwide evolution of global training has led us to focus on the management of a multiple-location system for the deployment of training and development, which can be thought of as a distribution network for corporate knowledge and training. Modern technology allows us to keep a virtual presence around the world while simultaneously using regional centers for personal contact in local offices. Regardless of the specifics, the primary concern of training and development systems is to improve performance, manage knowledge, and cultivate a quality culture.

This book will be useful to those who are responsible for distributing training and development across multiple locations and/or cultures as they struggle with ways to address these challenges while responding to both local clients and corporate managers. It includes some theory, but the focus is on the practice of the training and development function in organizations that are globalizing and have headquarter offices with divisional/regional centers in multiple markets, in multiple countries. This book contains models and paradigms, as well as illustrations and job aids, but the heart of the text is, of course, the many specific ideas for managing a multiple location training and development function.

We appreciate the patience of those who have been close to us during the period in which this writing took place, especially our spouses, Levirina Helena Krempl and Gae Tueller Pace. Jonathon Poh and Lori Figueiredo provided invaluable input into the initial thinking about the multiple-location system model. Janice Snow Lohmann contributed to the organization of the text and provided indispensable editing expertise. Dick Swanson offered kind and reasonable encouragement and provided excellent reviewers to clarify our thinking and focus our direction. Steve and Wayne met in Hawaii and created this work almost entirely via the World Wide Web as each labored in different parts of the universe, attending to their various professional commitments.

Stephen F. Krempl, Plano, Texas
R. Wayne Pace, St. George, Utah
February 2001

THE NATURE OF MULTIPLE-LOCATION T&D SYSTEMS

In general, we can say that the larger the system becomes, the more the parts interact, the more difficult it is to understand environmental constraints, the more obscure becomes the problem of what resources should be made available, and deepest of all, the more difficult becomes the problem of the legitimate values of the system.

C. WEST CHURCHMAN

Vast business opportunities in Asia, South America, Africa, and other parts of the world have enticed many companies to expand their marketing and manufacturing capabilities worldwide. Truly, we are in a global age. Organizations all over the world are rushing to develop global operations. Odenwald (1993) has noted that "corporate human resource executives are setting up training management teams in regions around the world" (p. 160). This global expansion requires multinational corporations to examine how they manage the increased complexity of training and development (T&D) operations that involve multiple locations. Thus, we will begin by discussing the goals and impact of globalization on a multiple-location training organization and the three dilemmas that every training manager in this environment must face. How do we balance the desire for autonomy with the need for some central control and standardization? Do we position training and development near the power centers or near the people they serve? Do we want our professional staff seen as business managers or learning specialists?

GLOBAL BUSINESS

Doing business globally is a tremendous undertaking for a company's internal business functions. Expanding beyond a company's primary market into new areas of the world involves dealing with diverse ethnic groups, multiple cultures, varied languages, and different business practices. These variables, coupled with local laws and restrictions, can make it difficult to establish effective work systems and processes. Developing and maintaining effective workers and business operations in this environment may be one of the most challenging opportunities that the new global economy provides. It can be a recipe for disaster.

To support employees dispersed worldwide, some companies are establishing regional support centers, which often include services for more than one company or product. For example, when PepsiCo managed Taco Bell, KFC, and Pizza Hut restaurants, its major regions (Asia, Europe, and South America) each had only one regional center. However, that regional center served all three companies. These support facilities ensured that PepsiCo consistently and efficiently delivered high-quality training, regardless of the company or region.

The T&D function must consider various distribution systems for delivering its products and services to multiple locations. Figure 1.1, which illustrates some typical distribution systems, assumes a corporate headquarters that disseminates general policies/information to distant offices. Five distribution channels are represented in Figure 1.1. A multinational or multilocation corporation could utilize any or all of these channels to distribute services, products, or information. Communication may occur as indicated by channel A, directly from corporate headquarters to employees; channel B, from corporate headquarters to divisional or regional centers and then to employees; or channel C, from corporate headquarters to markets, then to specific product outlets/stores and on to employees. D portrays a system in which policy/information is distributed from headquarters

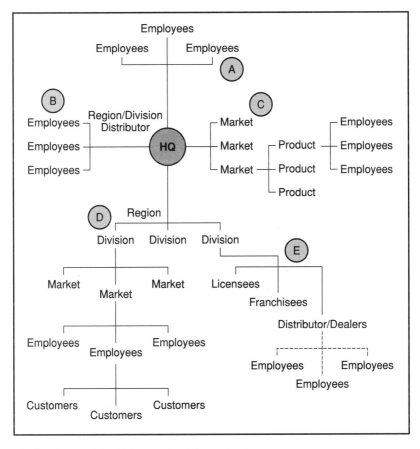

FIGURE 1.1 A Multiple-Location Distribution System

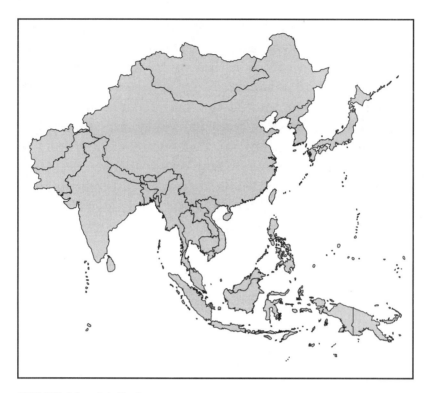

FIGURE 1.2   Asia Region

to a regional center, on to divisional sites, then market locations, then to employees, and finally to customers/users. E is a similar system but shows training being distributed from divisions to licensees, on to franchisees, dealer/distributors, and finally their employees. The dotted line emphasizes that these units are not legally part of the parent organization. In fact, as employees of a distributor or franchisee, they may not even be employees of the corporation. Nevertheless, they are a vital component in the distribution of training.

The key intermediate point in the B and D lines is the "'region'." There is no universally accepted definition of the term *region*. Nye (1968) explains, "There are no absolute or naturally determined regions. Relevant geographical boundaries vary with different purposes; for example, a relevant region for security may not be one for economic integration" (p. 75). Nevertheless, a region is one important unit in many multiple-location training distribution systems.

For the purpose of clarity, we will think of a region as a geographic area defined by distinct business activity. Regions usually encompass more than one state or country. We may refer to the Asian Region (Figure 1.2) or the Latin American Region. For instance, an Italian manufacturer may classify the entire United States as a region. Thus, a region often consists of business units operating under a single corporate headquarters within a definable geographical area in which the company conducts business.

GOALS OF A MULTIPLE-LOCATION T&D SYSTEM

The T&D function has mission-critical goals. Among them are (1) to manage knowledge distribution, (2) to establish/support a culture that spans national and local organizations and connects them to the corporate culture, and (3) to enhance individual performance and organizational capability.

Distribute and Manage Knowledge

The primary goal of any T&D organization is to manage the flow of knowledge within the corporation. This goal represents a greater challenge in a multilocation system. The challenge lies in trying to capture this knowledge from the far reaches of the corporation. Doing so requires a systematic way of identifying, capturing, encoding, and disseminating the information. This is already a significant task and will become more important over time.

Knowledge management deals with the way in which information is distributed and used in an organization (Herling & Provo, 2000). In general, information represents the sounds and movements people make and the electrical impulses of machines before we respond to them. It is the impersonal sounds, actions, and impulses directed our way, intentionally or not. For example, when we answer the telephone, we respond to information, in this case sounds, and then make sense out of them. When we make sense out of information, it becomes knowledge. Knowledge is generally defined as having direct awareness of something, making sense of information. It is a particularly human activity.

Managing knowledge means that someone directs, regulates, maintains, and influences the sense that is made of public information—that is, information that is available to all parties. Thus, if you manage knowledge, you have the ability to influence what information employees use to make decisions and guide actions. Since the T&D function directs what information is available and influences how employees translate that information into knowledge, they have a tremendous impact on knowledge flow.

If we understand that a person's perceptions are a function of the personal knowledge they have, then we can understand the immense responsibility we have for what people think and how they act. Every program, every contact that the T&D staff have with employees represents an opportunity to influence knowledge flow, which then influences individual performance and corporate capability.

Support or Enhance Culture

The second goal of the T&D function is to establish a culture that spans national and local organizations and connects them to the corporate culture. National culture consists of common perceptions and actions in a particular country. The most apparent aspects of a national culture are language, attitude toward time, use of space, and dominant religion.

Corporate culture is a system of shared beliefs and values that guide decisions and actions. T&D influences cultural issues as an outgrowth of knowledge transfer. As information enters our consciousness and sense making occurs, we store in our minds private knowledge, our special meanings. When we talk to others, private knowledge becomes public knowledge. Public knowledge about an organization—what we should do and how we should act—is the fabric of corporate culture. Since T&D distributes public knowledge, it follows that it is concerned with the culture of the organization. Thus, the T&D function must cultivate and maintain the culture, if the culture is to support the T&D function.

An organization's culture emerges from the collective experience of its members as they share symbols, rites, and rituals. Bolman and Deal (1991) refer to this as the "symbolic frame" and compare the organization to a theater in which each person takes a role. The costumes, stage setting, and acting (ways of talking and behaving) convey the meaning of the play (the organization) to both the actors and the audience.

Like a play, an organization has a story line that articulates what is important in the culture. Business attire and uniforms become costumes. The daily enactment of the script reveals the story, and the symbols reveal those things that are stable and enduring. The ultimate expression of the theatrical metaphor is manifest at Disney theme parks, where employees are "on stage" at all times. Although Disney locations have elaborate stage settings, costumes, and scripts, each is a real business, similar to other successful businesses. Indeed, Southwest Airlines and Merrill Lynch have their own cultures that are also fully consistent with the theatrical metaphor. You may want to examine your corporate culture in terms of what its stage, costumes, and scripts say.

A strong organizational culture cuts two ways. First, unique, shared values develop a vigorous corporate identity, enhance employee commitment, reduce the need for formal controls, and create a stable social system. However, it may become rigid and thus project a narrow perspective and create a restrictive environment. If dramatic changes need to be made in the organization, a strong culture may offer strong resistance to that change, making innovation and adaptation nearly impossible.

A strong and clearly defined culture can provide a distinct advantage for multiple-location systems. Many organizations want to present a common "face" to the customer. That "face" represents the culture and values of the organization. Giving everyone the same "face" requires training—employee training, business partner training, distributor training. Strong cultures may underlie some other paradoxes in managing the T&D function in multiple locations. So, how do you bridge the gap between a strong corporate culture and the distinct local or national cultures? What strategies would ensure that the best outcomes are reached? Organizations expect T&D to gather input and provide leadership in achieving this delicate balance.

Enhance Individual Performance and Organizational Capability

The third goal of the T&D function in multiple-location systems is to develop a baseline of common knowledge and skill that spans regions and is consistent with corporate expectations. Individual performance improvement is an important goal of any T&D function, but doing that within a system of dispersed multiple locations is a great challenge. Without regularly updated information, reinforced and refined, individuals in distant locations have a tendency to evolve personalized and idiosyncratic interpretations that affect their decisions and actions.

A multitude of distortions, errors, and biases may emerge from distributing information through human systems, all of which may affect the performance and ability of individuals and groups. Quality, relevance, timeliness, and amount of information are critical variables affecting how employees do their work. Without the best knowledge, employees cannot execute their work competently. However, competence is not enough.

Herling and Provo (2000) explain that

"having a competent workforce allows the organization to maintain its competitive position. To move the organization forward and grow requires highly knowledgeable and skilled individuals capable of solving progressively more difficult and unique situational problems. In short, sustained organizational success requires employee expertise, not just employee competence." (p. 5)

The ability of the T&D function to help employees access the knowledge necessary to enhance their existing abilities and develop expertise may determine the long-range success of the organization. In establishing a multiple-location system, T&D leaders may encounter common paradoxes that directly impact on the strategy they choose for their day-to-day operations.

PARADOXES IN MANAGING MULTIPLE-LOCATION T&D SYSTEMS

The nature of a multiple-location system lends itself to contradiction and paradox. The system has roots in a centralized organization such as corporate headquarters but must function in a local environment far removed and vastly different from the central unit. This paradigm gives rise to several questions. Where should T&D reside, and what criteria should be used to make that decision? Are T&D professionals primarily educators/trainers, or are they business thinkers whose venue is adult education and training? Who should control which aspects of the T&D function—corporate or regional? These issues must be explored as a multilocation system is designed.

Paradox 1: Business Managers versus Learning Specialists

Managers located in business units or operational units sometimes argue that T&D staff do not understand business or operational issues. They are educators. Thus, the operations function often establishes its own training unit charged with business, technical operations, or sales training. T&D, then, handles only management development, a nonbusiness responsibility. One way to address this paradox is for T&D staff to be fully informed about business issues. This allows the function to be based where it can achieve its goals most effectively, engage in the most effective knowledge management, develop the most appropriate organizational culture, and improve the performance and capability of both individuals and the organization.

Paradox 2: Power versus Proximity

As a general principle, the T&D function should be located where it has the most positional influence. If human resources is an established function that carries the right budget and political influence, then T&D should be located there. However, if operations is the strongest unit, it should be located with operations. Making the decision based on positional influence also means that T&D could report directly to the chief executive officer.

Always, however, T&D should be closely connected with the people so that it can work effectively on knowledge management, organizational culture, and performance and capability improvement. It needs to be "out there" in the field where the work is performed. But the centers of power are usually not in the field. How does T&D maintain a close connection with the power base and still be near the people? The means to this end are simple and inexpensive. The keys are communication and visibility. T&D must have constant contact with the centers of power and keep those in powerful positions well informed about what is happening in the function. By conscientious use of the regular communication channels such as written reports or status update meetings, T&D maintains a presence with upper management. A more sophisticated approach would be to draft an advisory council or advisory board from among internal and external stakeholders or request the opportunity to present your plans and progress at a senior management meeting. The goal is to ensure that all parts of the corporation understand what T&D is doing and its impact.

Paradox 3: Central Control versus Regional Autonomy

In widely dispersed, multiple-location organizations, the issue of who controls the creation and distribution of T&D materials can become a difficult question. The dimensions of this issue are portrayed in Figure 1.3. The x-axis shows types of information to be developed and distributed as part of T&D functions; the y-axis identifies the location or level at which development and distribution could occur. As you can see, corporate headquarters (y-axis) has control over core operating standards (x-axis). This represents the most closely held issue at the center of the multilocation system. However, note that the units and markets exercise little

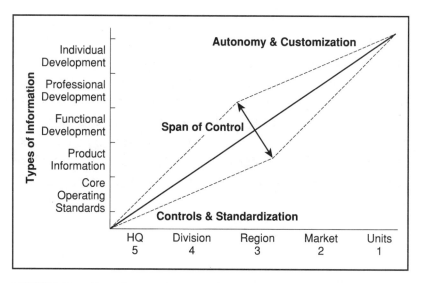

FIGURE 1.3   Control versus Autonomy Paradox

control over core operating standards. As you travel farther from this central issue, both organizationally and geographically, you begin to see how control of information shifts toward the regional level, with divisions and regions exercising greater control over product information and functional development. By the time you reach the market and unit levels, there is almost no control over core operating standards or product information, but extreme control over individual development issues. Thus, it may be inferred that in a multiple-location system there is both autonomy and control at work, but the issues over which each location exercises that control vary greatly, with corporate having more control over issues affecting the entire enterprise and units/markets dominating more individual and professional development. This makes sense as you look at the stakeholders in each area. As you study the chart, attempt to locate your situation in the matrix. You can then decide whether T&D materials should be handled somewhat differently in your organization.

The solid line running from left to right diagonally across the figure divides responsibilities of control and standardization from those of autonomy and customization. The dotted, arching lines indicate a zone of flexibility in which the decision to give up some control and provide more autonomy to subordinate units may happen. Corporate headquarters clearly controls the development and dissemination of core operating standards—little flexibility is evident here. However, as the chart shows, headquarters may relinquish control on such issues as product information, functional development, professional development, and individual development.

The issue of control versus autonomy in all forms of decision making permeates the relationship between headquarters staff and all others. The question becomes, To what extent can and should the multiple locations carry out their responsibilities independent of corporate headquarters? The answer to this question depends heavily on reporting relationships. In a multiple-location system that includes both domestic and international regions, the issue of who reports to whom and why is often critical.

Like the cycle of all things within organizations, the question will eventually be asked, "Why is the T&D function reporting to . . . ?" Or, when a realignment is announced, the question becomes "Where should the T&D function report?" Still, these questions are still better than asking, "Should the T&D function be eliminated or outsourced? If you've done your job, downsizing or eliminating the department and outsourcing the entire function should never happen. It is better for managers to argue about where it should report than to disregard it as it silently disappears.

Questions about where a department should report reflect concerns about control and efficiency. In some organizations, the T&D function reports to the operations groups; in some organizations, it reports to human resources. Technical trainers often report to operations, while management development specialists may report to human resources. In some cases, a third organization—a corporate training function, such as that at Motorola—is also responsible for training. This third group may have its own separate organization and facilities. In such cases, at least two, maybe three, training organizations exist at one time—a corporate university, a regional center, and a local business unit.

In a multiple-location system, the T&D function should ideally have corporate, regional, market, and unit representation that mirrors their organizations' structures. Such an arrangement helps resolve the control-versus-autonomy paradox by means of the division of activities between the corporate, region, market, and unit staffs. How responsibilities are divided may be analyzed by using the ADDIE model for instructional design (Gagne & Medsker, 1996; Swanson, 1996). Who does the needs analysis? Who does the instructional design? Who is responsible for courseware development? Program implementation? Who handles evaluation of T&D programs?

Are clear guidelines already established that spell out the nature of relationships among these different levels and among the tasks to be performed? If guidelines are in place and followed, changes may not be needed. If no policy guidelines exist, they must be created. Policy development can be organized around the types of programs to be offered. For example, corporate headquarters staff can develop leadership training programs; the region can develop managerial programs; the markets can develop supervisory programs. Or, development can be divided according to predetermined guidelines associated with the ADDIE tasks. For example, the analysis of training needs can be shared as corporate headquarters determines the kinds of information to be collected while regional staff actual collects the data. Headquarters can determine the scope of the analysis and regional staff can conduct the actual fieldwork. The data can then be consolidated at headquarters and disseminated to distant locations. An alternative would be to complete the analysis for any particular program at the market level, supervised by divisional/regional staff. Decisions concerning the other elements of ADDIE—design, development, implementation, and evaluation—should also be included in the policy statement as they provide a basis for decision making and allow each level to determine how it can contribute to goal achievement. The key here is the creation of a clear policy statement. Multiple-location systems must rely more on policy statements in the areas of ADDIE responsibilities to manage the widely distributed locations.

Any discussion of the control-versus-autonomy paradox must include a consideration of the extent to which T&D is centralized at the corporate level. Control is needed, but the three T&D goals are affected by how much and how it is administered. Too much control may negatively impact individual performance, splinter organizational culture, or cripple knowledge management. Nevertheless, the regional/divisional function must operate somewhat autonomously from the headquarters function, with headquarters supervision. The region/division should maintain supervisory control over ADDIE activities at the market and local levels. The primary objective of this control is to guard against duplication of effort and allow for identification of clear roles and responsibilities for all training units. An effective way to achieve this balance is to create a model that defines what remains centralized and what will be left to the autonomy of the locations.

CONCLUSION

The globalization of business has given rise to unparalleled opportunity tempered only by the risk inherent in failing to manage the people and processes needed to fully utilize that opportunity. For the training and development function, the risk lies in failing to reach the mission-critical goals of managing knowledge in multiple locations, supporting diverse cultures, and enhancing performance across geographic and national boundaries. But the very nature of a multiple-location system embodies paradoxes that challenge even the best management talent. Are we seen as business managers or learning specialists? Do we position ourselves closer to the people or closer to the power? How do we attain the most effective balance between control and autonomy? The answer lies in adherence to a system encompassing all aspects of the training and development process. Toward that goal, the traditional training model, ADDIE, can be applied in a larger way to create and manage a multiple-location system. Chapter 2 will expand on this theme and discuss in detail how ADDIE can be used as part of the framework for building the multiple-location system.

CHAPTER 2

A MODEL FOR CREATING A MULTIPLE-LOCATION T&D SYSTEM

It is best to do things systematically, since we are only human, and disorder is our worst enemy.

HESIOD

A multiple-location T&D system can be characterized as a set of building blocks, with each block representing one aspect of the department. In this chapter we will describe this system and its components as viewed from two major perspectives: the training and development perspective and the business perspective. As seen in Figure 2.1, the system can be modeled after the classic ADDIE development process, covering all aspects from analysis to evaluation. For the system to stand as designed, each building block must be in place and held together with the "glue" of political savvy, which we will discuss in Chapter 7. If one block is missing, the structure is weakened.

THE TRAINING AND DEVELOPMENT PERSPECTIVE

The classic ADDIE process used for designing individual programs can be adapted to the design of a multiple location T&D system. As you learned in Chapter 1, the acronym

ADDIE describes five steps in the instructional design process: analysis, design, development, implementation, and evaluation. From the training perspective, the upward arrows (Fig. 2.1) on the left side of the model summarize the process. It begins on the bottom row of blocks with an analysis (A) of the organization's needs. The next row of blocks represents designing (D) an intervention or plan to respond to those needs. The third row of blocks represents developing (D) the tools to support the plan. The fourth stage entails implementing (I) the plan, and, finally, the fifth stage is evaluating (E) the results. Using a framework like ADDIE provides T&D professionals with a familiar framework for thinking about how to build a multiple-location organization. However, it is not the only perspective.

THE BUSINESS PERSPECTIVE

The traditional business perspective is also reflected in Figure 2.1. The upward arrows on the right side of the model summarize the business or systems approach. So from that perspective, the process also begins with the *analysis/ business input phase,* which again is the bottom row of building blocks. Like all the rows of blocks after it, this one is composed of processes and activities that are essentially the same whether viewed from a T&D perspective or a business perspective. The ADDIE model tends to apply the processes to the limited environment of a training intervention, whereas the business perceptive applies them to the broader organizational setting. Thus, the analysis label refers to analyzing a target audience for a specific program(s). The business input process is much the same applied to a larger scale and scope.

Moving up the model, the next rows of blocks are the *design/organizational structure phase* and the *development/*

FIGURE 2.1 The Building Blocks of a Multiple-Location T&D System: Analysis/Business Input Phase

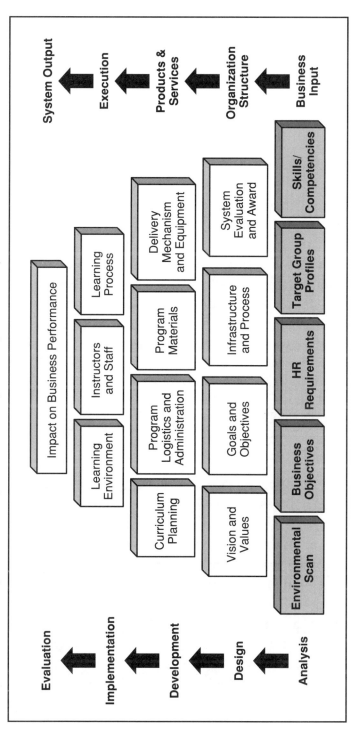

products and services phase. Again, design and development can apply only to developing a training intervention, or they can apply to designing and developing the organizational structure, product, and services that deliver training intervention. The *implementation/execution phase* involves considerations of the human element and quality control, and, finally, the *evaluating/system output phase* measures the effect of the first four rows. Viewing the process from the business perspective provides business-oriented individuals with a familiar framework. Only viewing the process from both perspectives yields a true picture of the value added by training and development. T&D is both education and business; it speaks to knowledge management and skill development. The two views adequately address the concerns of those who would say that training is just education. As the model shows, it is both—and a multiple-location system must be created taking into account both perspectives.

THE ADDIE PROCESS

Phase 1: Analysis/Business Input

From the T&D perspective, analysis is action you take to determine what the target audience needs to achieve their program goals. This includes identifying skill, knowledge, and performance gaps that can be closed with training interventions and job aids. The same principle can be applied to formulate plans for a multiple-location system. Since the ultimate goal is to close existing performance gaps, the process begins with determining the needs of your target audience (e.g., general managers, divisional or regional leaders, or local employees). The analysis phase (Fig. 2.1, bottom row of blocks) is the foundation of the system because understanding issues and problems must precede the design and development of products and services to enhance performance capability.

The T&D system must be based on the business direction of the company, which is made up of the market or business plans of its units and separate companies. You need to secure the consolidated business plans of all units in the multiple-location chain that you serve. This information may be most available from the corporate headquarters. Study the plans to identify the variables that drive business plans and reveal regional or country-specific differences. As part of the analysis, company business plans and long-term strategic plans for the different units should be reviewed to set the goals for the T&D function.

Developing a total plan requires gathering information on each of the five elements of business input shown in Figure 2.1 and knowing what they reveal about the business units. The five elements are (1) the environmental scan, (2) specific business objectives, (3) human resource requirements, (4) target group profile, and (5) skill and competence requirements. Each of these deserves a detailed examination.

Environmental Scan

The environmental scan deals with information about the social and economic variables of each country, division, or region. It also is concerned with the trends in your industry that have an impact on your business in those locations. For example, the environmental scan may show changes in competitor activities that could affect your business. If competitors are using new modes of distribution, communication, or technology, you should determine what potential effects those changes have on the way you deliver or distribute your products or services. This is important as staff retraining might be required to catch up with the competition.

PESTLE Analysis Table 2.1 shows how the results of an environmental scan may be portrayed for rapid analysis and decision making. The six primary elements are listed down the left-hand side of the table: political, economic, social, technological, legal, and environmental (PESTLE). From the data gathered, the sample PESTLE chart reveals the key conclusions drawn in terms of the market or the corporation and the T&D function. Notice how the T&D function is affected by the status of each of the six PESTLE factors.

Regarding the political climate, imminent elections often create turmoil among local populations. If the situation turns violent, the ensuing disruption can affect business. In Table 2.1, the political climate appears stable, which means that T&D can move toward being more widely recognized as a business partner in that country's operations. At the same time, social conditions are sufficiently stable to allow active recruitment and employment of foreign workers. While each variable in the PESTLE analysis may not be an issue in each country or market, each one should be considered to provide opportunity for thorough analysis. It is best to consolidate all new initiatives within the targeted geographic area and arrange them into meaningful categories using the PESTLE format. As the area leader, you should have the resources and authority to request information from units in the division, region, and markets. As Chapter 7 will indicate, being involved in information gathering and planning meetings strengthens your credibility in the organization.

The prevailing government's view of corporations and their foreign national employees is important in maintaining workable relationships. When building a T&D function in another country, establishing and maintaining good relations with local government officials is desirable so you can hire those who speak the local language and demonstrate

TABLE 2.1 Country PESTLE Analysis

	Macro (Market level)	Micro (Organizational level)	Micro (T&D Department)
Political	Stable	Stable	T&D now being recognized as a business partner by other departments
Economic	Recession Increased spending on fast food	Aggressive sales targets	Annual plans and budget approved
Social	Increased trend in employing foreign workers	Overseas recruitment to attract foreign workers	T&D team not in place Trainees profiles changing from local to foreign workers
Technological	Competitors introducing Smart Card	Limited computer infrastructure in	Limited computer infrastructure in the T&D Department
Legal	Changing health regulations	Reviewing changes needed to meet new health regulations	Training required on the new health regulations
Environmental	Food industry challenged to be more environmentally friendly	No priority placed on environmental issues	No priority placed on environmental issues

strong cultural skills. The ability to assimilate and cooperate effectively improves if you understand and acknowledge local practices, business nuances, and cultural norms.

As part of the environmental scan, you also need to identify and categorize the different markets and regions so you can target those that have greater potential. Some markets are mature and slowing, while others are growing rapidly. Recognizing these differences makes the most appropriate investment of your company's T&D dollars and your time. This is part of the business sense that should be acquired by T&D personnel. A quick look at the business numbers might be enlightening.

In many industries, profit and loss numbers change in a matter of months. Thus, strategic plans for markets should serve as the primary basis for developing priorities for the T&D function in the short term. Beyond establishing priorities, the other important point—no matter what time frame is used, whether months or weeks—is how the T&D function responds to demands, opportunities, and challenges implied in the scan.

Another source of information is the annual organizational capability and human resource needs review. It provides data about the status of personnel throughout the organization, so you can derive insights into the strengths and developmental needs of employees. In fact, you may get some ideas about the effectiveness of various T&D functions throughout the organization and what they are doing to support their organizational goals and achieve business objectives.

Although the environmental scan helps you track global training trends and technology in the industry, how technology affects the design, delivery, and distribution of training through the organization is extremely important. Chapter 4 addresses some of these issues, providing examples of how some companies use technology to distribute training or solve problems. Although every method is not appropriate for every organization, you should be aware of the different methodologies and their effectiveness in diverse industries and cultures.

Market Profile Another part of the environmental scan is the market profile. As Table 2.2 shows, many factors affect the selection of development interventions and the scope of work in a market. For instance, training a large number of employees from one company-owned unit, all of whom work in a manufacturing environment, is a very different assignment from training the same number of employees working in both sales and manufacturing in franchise/distributor environments. First, you must consider all the same variables you would consider for any training program (e.g., education, skill set, outcomes, business issues, etc.). However, in a multiple-location system, you must then consider specific issues such as language and setting. What language do the targeted employees speak? Do they also speak another language well enough for training to take place in either language? How about reading? In some remote manufacturing locations, you might not be able to assume that employees can read. However, you would probably not have that concern if they were located in a more developed country. These considerations also affect selection of training materials used.

In addition to language issues, often ownership issues affect training. If the targeted group works in a company-owned facility and are employees of the organization, you might have more latitude in what and how you teach. If they are employees of a franchise or distributor, you may be required to train them, but you are more limited in what you can mandate. In such cases, political skill can be as important to getting your goals met as professional competence.

TABLE 2.2 Market Profile

Market	Business Unit	Company Owned	Franchise/distributors	Joint Venture	Percentage Business Growth	Number of Staff	Language(s)	Business Issues
1	Sales	Yes	No	No	30	30	English	Skilled labor
	Manufacturing	No	No	No				
	Customer Support	Yes	No	No		100		
2	Sales	Yes	Yes	No	128	50	Mandarin	Largest
	Manufacturing	No	No	No			English	growth
	Customer Support	Yes	No	No		150		planned
3	Sales	No	No	No	50		German	Highly
	Manufacturing	Yes	No	Yes		3,500		competitive
	Customer Support	Yes	No	Yes				

SWOT Analysis The final step in an environmental scan is to draw overall conclusions about the threats to and strengths, weaknesses, and opportunities of each unit. Figure 2.2 shows how the four elements of a SWOT analysis can be used in understanding the competitive posture of the unit being analyzed. Finally, through the assessment of these business inputs, you should be able to create a vision of the role of the T&D function in your organization in preparing employees to adapt, cope, and change for the future.

Business Performance Objectives

The second building block is business performance objectives. Objectives are most clearly revealed in the strategic plans issued by your company's headquarters. They are

Strengths	Weaknesses
• Young dynamic team • High potential growth • High profit margins • Strong regional support	• No standards systems in place in most functions • Lack of discipline in following systems • Poor internal communication • Lack of required human resources for growth
Opportunities	**Threats**
• Increase in popularity of fast food • Kids marketing • To be recognized as the leading fast food brand	• Labor shortage • Industry not attracting high-caliber people • More local and international competitors

FIGURE 2.2 SWOT Analysis

usually published in the form of annual operating plans or in three- to five-year strategic plans. Many organizations also issue periodic reviews that show changes occurring throughout the company. These plans indicate issues that might have implications for the T&D function. Examples of typical issues are the number of new product launches, aggressive sales growth, expansion into new markets, and impending corporate franchising, mergers, or sales. Table 2.3 illustrates how certain business objectives may impact the T&D function. For example, a planned 50 percent increase in business outlets implies that the T&D function must plan for increased new-hire training and development.

Information about business performance objectives should help you understand the key performance objectives for various locations in the organization. At this point, you need to determine the role each of the locations that have T&D functions should play in achieving these business objectives. Although you may have, at this point, little to say about what the headquarters' T&D func-

TABLE 2.3 Business Performance Objectives

Business Performance Objectives for the Next 1 to 3 Years	Issues for T&D to Consider
Aggressive growth targets—50% increase in stores	Building the capabilities of current and new staff to support the growth
Roll out customer tracking and feedback system	Conduct system train-the-trainer sessions
Customer service program	Conduct needs analysis and source/develop relevant training programs

tion plans to do, if nothing else, a clear vision of what you are able and willing to do will give you some ideas about how to direct your discussions with senior management. Planning ahead allows you to prepare for constraints that might develop in allocating resources to key projects that assist the organization to meet its goals.

Human Resource Requirements

So far we have talked about two foundational tasks associated with business inputs that are essential to establishing a multiple-location T&D system—conducting an environmental scan and identifying business objectives. The third task is to discover the human resource requirements for the multiple-location system. Now that you have a better idea of both local and corporate business objectives, your next task is to assess and articulate the human resource requirements for the multiple locations. For example, based on information about the general capability of a region obtained from your needs analysis, you must now dig deeper into the personnel requirements.

Begin by determining how many employees you have in the various business units at both operational and management levels and in functional areas, such as manufacturing, information systems, warehousing, distribution, human resources, finance, and engineering. Assess both current and future human resource needs by studying data from the HR managers and information systems before securing an estimate of future projections.

Out of the human resource requirements come the primary human resource objectives for both the immediate year and the next three years. Table 2.4 illustrates the relationship between human resource objectives and the role of the T&D function in achieving the objectives. For example, the objective to recruit more foreign workers places a demand to review the profile of new employees

TABLE 2.4 Human Resource Objectives

HR Objectives/Initiatives for the Next 1 to 3 Years	T&D's Role
Implementing a systematic HR performance management process	Train each level of management to execute their part in the process
Increase in recruitment of foreign workers	Understand target group profile and determine whether current and future training approach needs to be adapted
Greater capabilities required at senior management level to be able to manage the rapid growth	Identify the additional training required by management

and determine whether changes should be made in approaches to T&D. At the same time, with increased numbers of foreign workers, the demand to have qualified managers also increases. Thus, shifts in human resource requirements and specific objectives and initiatives affect the role of the T&D function in achieving the objectives. Information about human resource requirements should also come from managers of each level in the organization. The priorities of the business operations managers are very important, especially for political reasons since, as discussed in Chapter 7, it's wise to determine how your views match those of local managers as well as those of headquarters.

Finally, the basic question for the T&D function relates to what you see as the role of the T&D function in meeting the human resource requirements of the organization. If the business operations include franchise units, a joint venture partner, or other business partners, then you might have to consider how you can assist them in light of resource limitations.

Target Group Competency Profiles
Based on the analysis of human resource requirements, the next step is to determine the general development needs for each target group in each location and their order of priority. Arriving at this decision requires a profile of each potential target group (Table 2.5). The various locations should provide you with this information by function, organizational level, relevant experience, education completed, cultural background, and languages spoken and written. This raises some questions. What is the gap between current and required competencies of personnel in each market? How should we meet the short- and long-term performance requirements and business needs? Which needs can be met at the corporate level, and which should be met at other levels?

Profiling each employee or target group in each location allows the T&D function to identify learning and performance needs affecting outcomes. For example, in Asia there might be a need to learn broad business skills due to rapid growth, but in other locations the need might be for the acquisition of first-line supervisory skills.

Target Group Competence Requirements
Special attention should be focused on the capabilities of management groups identified in the previous step. This is strategic information, as the management level not only receives training and development but influences access to employees they supervise. Furthermore, individual competencies determine who needs more T&D time and support. Competence gaps are derived from the business input process or as you complete a comprehensive competency assessment. For instance, imagine that

TABLE 2.5 Target Group Profiles

Target Group	Region/ Market	Total Number	Average Tenure	Key Roles	Programs Available	Programs Planned	Priority
Sales	Asia	50	2	Prospecting	Sales 101 101, 102 102, 103 201	104 consulting skills	C
	Europe	75	5	Prospecting vs. major account management	201, 202 201		
	United States	350	8	Building relationships	None		
Trainers	China	30	2	Field training	Need trans- lated version of 202		B
	U.K.	20	4	Field training & development			
	Brazil	15	1	Field training			
Engineer	Europe	450	5	Need new "black belt" skills		"Black belt" certification to be developed/ purchased ASAP	A
	Asia	350	5				
	United States	1,000	8				

one target audience is engineers. Through the business-input process, you discover that the corporation will introduce new technology next year. As you investigate further, you discover that engineers within a specific region have little or no expertise in using this new technology. Since this is a high-priority initiative, they must be trained to use it.

The ideal scenario is to build a competency profile of the different target audiences in your company and measure gaps against the profile. The specifics of conducting a competency analysis are readily available in many books and programs and are not covered here. Having a competence plan will guide the user and his or her manager in determining how much development time to anticipate, what development activities to arrange for, and how to measure the results.

This kind of planning invariably leads to a discussion regarding what portion of the development activities should handled by the headquarters T&D function and what portion should be handled by other levels in the organization, such as by regional T&D teams or local unit managers and staff. These decisions should be based on overall priorities and the mission statements of T&D units at the various company levels. In addition, the individual capabilities of T&D personnel should be compared against required needs to determine who should be assigned to participate.

Another factor to consider in making decisions about providing T&D services is whether support can be solicited from a local college, university, local training companies, and/or local consultants. In many cases, a worldwide arrangement with a large consulting group, such as STS International, or with training companies, such as Provant, Inc., might be a viable solution.

Having reached the end of the analysis/business input phase, you have now identified the general characteristics of the multiple locations involved in the system, the goals of the business, the target populations, and their competencies. The next phase of development concerns the structure of the T&D function in a multiple-location context. During this phase, you will design an organization and create the infrastructure for it.

Phase 2: Design/Organizational Structure

Once the analysis/business input phase has been completed, the next step is to design the system that will meet the identified needs. The framework for the function can be defined in advance and then systematically put into place over a predetermined time frame, depending on what seems appropriate for achieving company goals. As the T&D function leader, you must have a two-year plan in mind.

In the traditional ADDIE model, the design phase (Fig. 2.3, second row of blocks) is used to blueprint the intervention that will close the performance gap identified in the need analysis. However, when using ADDIE to create a multiple-location T&D system, the design is broader and encompasses designing the system itself, from vision to evaluation. The blocks on the second row represent the elements of the design/organizational structuring process vision and value, goals and objectives, infrastructure and process, system evaluation, and award. Activities at this stage require not only deciding current requirements but also projecting future needs.

Vision and Values

The first task is to identify the corporate position on the T&D function, to secure a statement of its specific purpose. However unusual, the corporate mission statement might not include a statement about the T&D function. If so, the corporate function to which T&D ultimately reports should issue a statement specifically stating its

FIGURE 2.3 Multiple-Location System Model: Design/Organizational Structure Phase

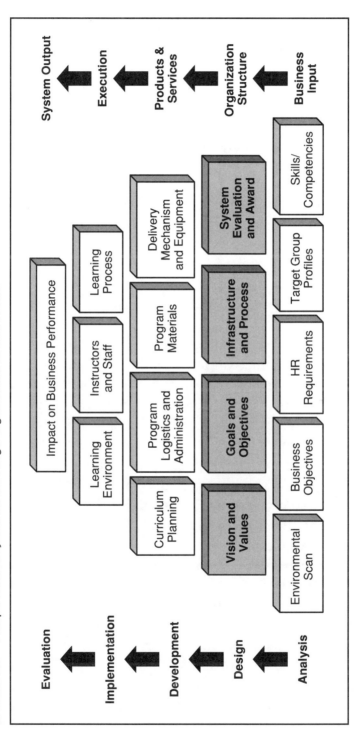

position toward T&D units at the divisional, regional, and market levels. Such a statement makes public the reasons for having a T&D function at those levels of the organization. It could also state the company goals for T&D across the entire organization. A clear corporate statement allows managers in widely distributed locations to articulate why the T&D function exists there.

Any statement of vision and values should capture why the current T&D strategy is the best way to approach the development of employees. For example, development might be part of the current company culture, belief and history, or the result of a new effort to develop workers' capabilities. A vision and values statement might be "To develop the capability of employees so the products and services they create and provide are the choice of discriminating buyers."

The vision statement includes information about possible future accomplishments of the department. It also identifies the kind of organization that should be created and paints a picture of what the organization will look like in the future. If your company has a worldwide vision for the T&D function, you might already have some language that supports the higher ideals of the organization. A vision statement for a regional or market T&D function might be "To be recognized throughout the company as a department that nurtures a world-class learning system that serves as a model of excellence for other units."

Values express the function's guiding principles in terms of thinking, actions, and decisions that are most important in moving the T&D unit toward the one described in the vision. The values become very useful, especially when you have staff, vendors, and other external contacts you would like to behave in accordance with your values. Values give customers a clear feel for how they should treat and interact with members of your team and employees in general.

A value statement might be phrased like this: "To respect all employees equally, to understand and respond to the true needs of customers, to be professional in thoughts and actions, and to provide goods and services with complete integrity."

Whatever the actual statements look like, they represent two or three pages that show what the function is, why it exists, and how it will operate within the company. As you phrase the vision and values statement, think about how others will interpret the statement and whether they will actually agree with it. You may want to involve others in creating the purpose statement; otherwise, you will need to develop a campaign to sell it to the organization. Involving others is a much easier way to create aligned visions.

Goals and Objectives

The second element of the organizational structure is the goals and objectives, which follow from its vision and values. Goals and objectives should clearly indicate what kinds of products and services are to be provided and state your intention to achieve the business or market's key performance objectives. The issue involves deciding what needs to be done to help accomplish company objectives.

Department objectives can be derived from information included in the business input where the question "What role should T&D play in achieving the business and human resource objectives?" was answered. The department is going to prepare employees for the initiatives and changes occurring in the environment and meet the development needs of specific target groups. The goals and objectives of the T&D function should reveal those intentions.

Objectives should be stated in very specific terms so anyone can tell how and when the objectives were achieved. For example, the general manager should be able to recognize when the number of products manufactured achieves the business objectives. The manager should know how many widgets must be prepared and sold to make a profit that contributes to the company's overall competitiveness. When objectives are definitively stated so that the productivity actually needed to achieve them is clear, the objectives are measurable. For example:

- to create a company-wide framework for use in providing workplace learning experiences,
- to provide interpersonal and technical support to T&D units,
- to provide technical support for the delivery and facilitation of learning, and
- to align T&D decisions and actions with corporate and client group objectives.

Infrastructure and Process

The organization's infrastructure is key to meeting the goals and objectives you establish. An inadequate infrastructure can imperil goal attainment. Building an adequate infrastructure involves analyzing the work to be done from the perspective of basic business functions and then engaging in a three-step process to build the plan.

Step 1: Based on the needs assessment, project how many programs you will present during the fiscal year and what materials you will produce for them. Based on this, how much revenue can you expect to generate by charging for programs or materials? How much funding will the corporation or internal client groups allocate to the T&D function? Will it grow or remain flat? What other sources of revenue exist? Will the organization approve a fee-for-service arrangement with internal client groups? How about external clients?

Step 2: Based on the needs assessment and approved budget, build an organization to support development needs in client groups. The staff required will probably include one or more program designers, administers, and trainers. If a limited budget dictates a smaller staff, consider outsourcing specific projects, use outside training vendors, or identify independent contractors that would be available on a retainer basis for regular use until an increased head count can be obtained. Ask yourself these questions: How many staff do you need to make good on your promises? Must a large organization be created, or can the work be contracted out? Can internal assignments be rotated to have adequate staff, and could local interns be used to do part of the work?

Step 3: Finally, begin building a budget based on the ideal structure and submit it. Most people are too idealistic, and it takes a year or two before the training organization actually sees some results, especially if it is a new setup. The more your dollars spent can be measured against organizational results, the easier it will be to add staff.

Evaluation System and Awards

The final building block in the design/organizational structure phase is to set up a way to evaluate the effectiveness of the entire multiple-location system as opposed to measuring the effectiveness of individual programs. The purpose of evaluation is to provide clear evidence that the activities have been completed according to the set criteria. One way to evaluate is to have a set of questions that probe each area in the model. If employees performing the activities have clearly defined guidelines about what should be done, it is easier to find a way of evaluating the activities. Thus, an assessment instrument and process have been developed and are described in detail in Chapter 6. Evaluation, in the traditional ADDIE design process, is the phase in which products and services are judged to be achieving the organization's objectives. In the same manner, the effectiveness of the total system must be evaluated in terms of how well it functions and contributes to achieving company goals.

The evaluation system centers around a review document that is designed to measure the extent to which a T&D function is performing all the roles and responsibilities associated with a highly effective function. The results indicate where dips in performance, knowledge deficiencies, and cultural barriers present problems. The questions parallel the blocks in the system model. That is, each process represented by a building block also has a set of questions in the review document. Thus the audit is based entirely on the multiple-location system model discussed in this chapter. The review document itself can be used across countries, regions, and markets. Furthermore, it is easily deployed and completed using the Internet (see Chapter 6).

Phase 3: Development/Products and Services

The primary task of the multiple-location T&D organization is to develop the capability of employees and business units for the long run. Knowing the strengths of your various locations staff, as well as managers and employees in the markets (through your review audit), you begin to identify the T&D needs of the total organization. In the traditional ADDIE design process, the development stage (Fig. 2.4, third row of blocks) is where you start to build programs. Appropriate materials are created or collected, and relevant resources are gathered and carefully woven into a pattern of offerings that has a powerful impact.

Precisely the same process is used when you start to build the multiple-location T&D function into a system to achieve company goals. The highest standards should be

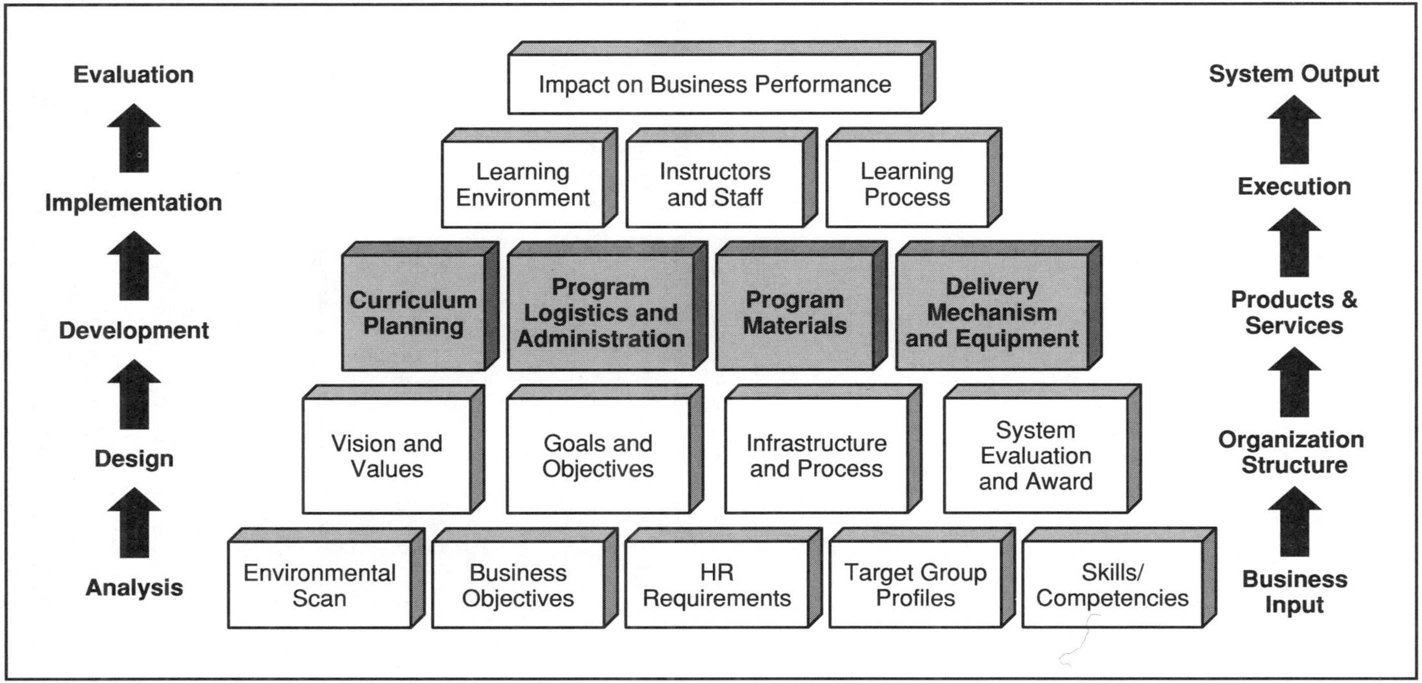

FIGURE 2.4 Multiple-Location System Model: Development/Products and Services Phase

set for each function in the system so a strong case can be built for securing the best resources at each level. The quality of resources ultimately determines the kind of support the T&D function can provide for business units. To build a complete T&D system from scratch usually takes two or three years. However, if you have many elements already in place, completing it within a year is not unreasonable.

While training programs are not the entirety of the T&D business, they are a large part of it. Certainly, most staff effort and budgets revolve around products and services, including training programs. Therefore, it is essential that every program be predicated on real needs.

Curriculum Planning

A *learning map* or *core curriculum* is a matrix of defined programs and organizational positions that show how the programs provide development for all levels of staff. This allows the markets or regional centers to have an overall picture of the development activities that are going on in that region, allowing one person to keep track of the total activities at the regional level. This process provides for a mechanism for capturing the overall picture of training and development in the organization.

All things equal, at least two training approaches (operations and management development) exist at the market level. Regardless of other issues, the capability of staff leading the T&D function at all levels usually determines the scope of the work and what can be accomplished. Table 2.6 illustrates organizing a learning map. Learning maps may also be organized around functions in the business units.

Program Logistics and Administration

Electronic training distribution systems are discussed in detail in Chapter 4. However, it is worthwhile to mention them here as technology is available in the marketplace to

TABLE 2.6 Curriculum Map

	VPs/General Managers	Market Managers	Functional Managers	Area Managers	Unit Managers
Orientation course	X	X	X	X	X
Functional course A		X	X		
B		X	X		
C		X	X		
Personal leadership course	X	X	X	X	
Business leadership course	X	X	X	X	X
• Advanced					
• Intermediate					
• Basic					
Organizational leadership course	X	X	X	X	X
Regional/university-based course	X	X	X		

help organizations streamline T&D administrative demands. However, the important question concerns what might be the ideal situation regarding the use of technology in handling the administrative details of a T&D function, especially one that involves multiple locations. Let us describe a possible scenario that represents many of the technological innovations on the horizon.

You walk into the office Monday morning, turn on the computer, and it reminds you to send feedback to participants who were involved in programs thirty, sixty, and ninety days ago. It highlights all activities for the week and the month to come. The computer confirms the instructors through e-mail and sends reminders to participants. It confirms their hotel reservations and activity schedule, and it sends materials for reproduction for the programs offered this week.

Here is the question you need to answer: Which of these administrative activities do you want to automate, and which ones do you want to administer yourself? This is an era in which most routine administrative activities can be completed by computer. Are you in a position to let a computer take care of these duties and free the training staff to create business-based, exciting training programs?

Program Materials

From a content standpoint, subject matter experts (SMEs) are one of the most important resources for multiple-location T&D staff. SMEs often provide critical information about best practices and local customs. However, one issue to consider is the availability of SMEs to invest in the development cycle. Another issue is whether the performance improvement and learning materials are customized and culturally adapted or come from standardized materials created by a corporate level development team. T&D staff who are close to local markets should have responsibility for deciding what materials need to be translated for various markets. Even though materials may be designed and marketed in English or received from headquarters in English, many in the target audience might prefer to receive information in their native language. The T&D manager and staff might also be required to deliver training in more than one language. Who is going to do the translation?

Another potential issue is how to pay for training design. Does corporate headquarters provide the staff with a budget? Do the markets pay for training design, or does someone else buy the design services for the T&D function in the field? Organizations handle these issues in various ways.

Many training programs are available over the Internet, especially at the level required for most entry-level employees or new managers. The potential for Internet training increases every year. With computer equipment available for most employees today, it is conceivable that training can be done at times that interfere least with the workday and in a very flexible way. The content available ranges from technical to interpersonal and management topics. The cost for some programs is incredibly low, some for as little as under $10 for a thirty-minute interactive session.

The T&D function will be well served to create a consistent look and feel for their development materials. Handouts, student handbooks, and instructors' guides can share the same style, colors, format, and so forth. Titles can share a similar style or design. Web-based training and CD-ROM labels can have the same look. This branding raises the visibility and improves the recognizability and image of the T&D function. Setting aside a shelf to showcase materials helps others see the contribution the department makes

In the same way, creating a template for student handbooks and instructor's guides actually aids development, decision making, effort and development time, and it cuts costs. The tendency in materials development is to begin thinking at the development/products and services phase. But you want to begin thinking about materials during the needs assessment process as it has implications for every other phase of development. For instance, information derived from the creation of the target profiles during the analysis/business input phase will assist you in modifying materials to various target audiences. It may be useful to store programs on CDs to aid in their retrieval and distribution. A Web site can be used as a real-time update tool to keep your clients aware of any schedule changes. Also, look into using the Web to handle registration and feedback to your clients.

Delivery Mechanisms and Equipment

Once training programs and materials are prepared, the next step is delivering them. How many services will the training staff offer? Other than the manager, who is going to provide the services? Even if the manager has the skills to deliver training, it might not be an advisable use of time. If the manager spends more than 30 percent of his or her time training, no time may be left to influence key decision makers and meet with customers.

The manager is primarily responsible for providing support rather than doing this work. Thus, line managers and local employees can offer services at the local level. An important consideration is the extent of their training skills and abilities, including the capability to deliver programs in the local language. Another critical consideration is the ability at the region or division level to provide train-the-trainer programs to enhance the abilities of local employees to assist with training. It is also possible to use contract trainers, assuming that they have sufficient knowledge and skill and that funds to pay them are available.

Phase 4: Implementation/Execution

Implementation, in the traditional ADDIE design process, is the phase in which products and services begin to be delivered to markets. Implementation involves translating the analysis, design, and development plans into deliverable products and services. The choice of environment, processes, and people should be based on the organization's vision and capability to deliver products and services. Implementation also involves consulting with units in the system on how to improve performance, manage knowledge, enhance the culture, and share information about best practices.

Learning Environment

The products, services, and support systems needed to deliver the T&D program are in place. Now they must be implemented in a way that is consistent with corporate philosophy and results in quality execution (Fig. 2.5, implementation/execution). The first step in the implementation phase is to create a learning environment that communicates to employees, vendors, and management the values, culture, priorities, expectations, and other messages of the organization. Thus, whether classroom or computer based, the learning environment should be true to the culture of the larger corporation while providing the optimal setting for learning. The Learning Center at Southwest Airlines in Dallas, Texas, is a good example of a learning environment that is faithful to the messages of the corporation.

Southwest Airlines is known as an employee-friendly organization. Throughout the corporation, the work environment is casual, fun, and characterized by positive energy. The culture encourages shared decision making, innovative problem solving, and teamwork. The training

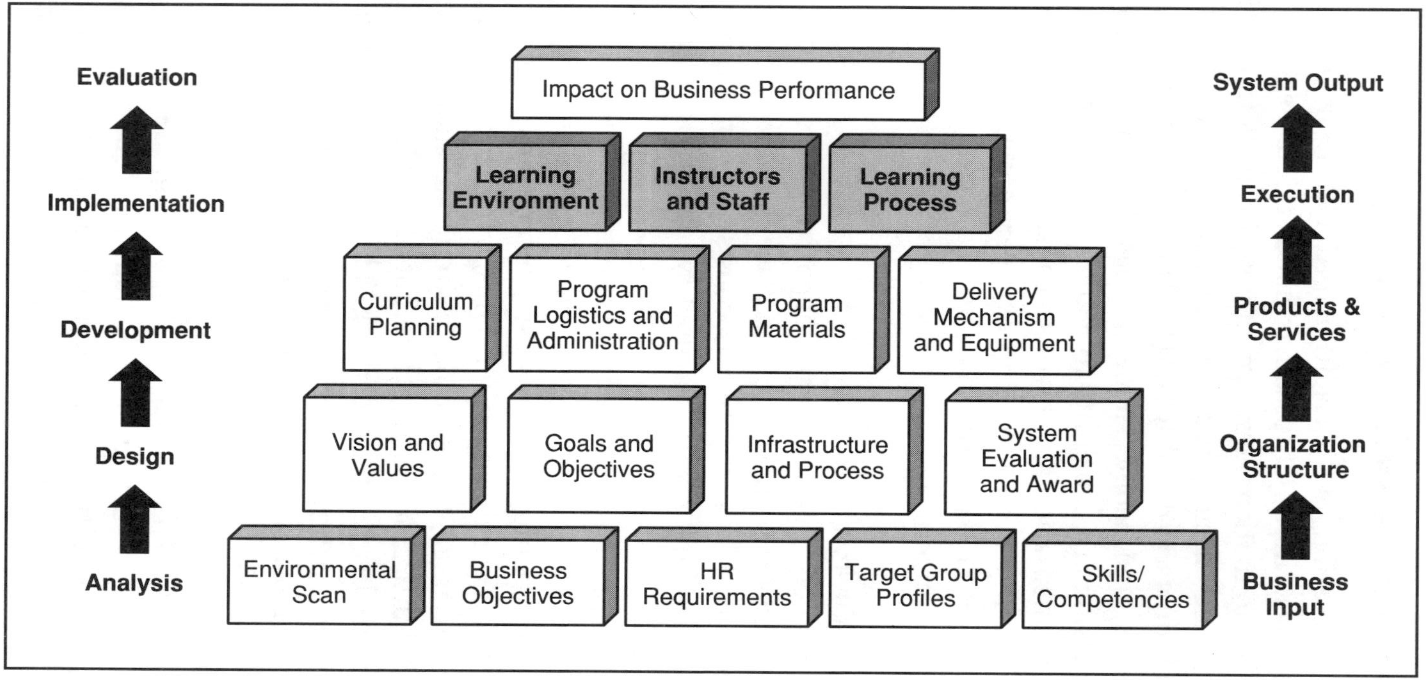

FIGURE 2.5 Multiple-Location System Model: Implementation/Execution Phase

center radiates this same message. The walls are colorful with handwritten messages from previous students. An aquarium housing tropical fish and plants decorates one wall. Music plays in the background. Classroom methodology contains liberal amounts of group activity with shared decision-making and teamwork. Clearly, the training center at Southwest Airlines reflects the culture and values of the parent organization.

The implementation of an environment sending the right messages requires detailed and advance thinking, careful planning, and constant monitoring. Figure 2.6 shows one of several checklists used in conjunction with the T&D system to guide a training manager on how to structure the appropriate learning environment. Since the implementation/execution phase is operationally oriented, it lends itself to the development of checklists as tools.

The tool in Figure 2.6 reflects the importance of considering all learning environments, not just those found in the traditional classroom. Thus, the environment for computer-based training is also important. The physical environment in which the learner resides during coursework is not the only environment. The courseware itself presents an environment. How does the learning package present on the screen? What about music? Is there a theme? Do users navigate themselves through the lessons, or is there an animated guide? The learner is surrounded by various environments in which the T&D staff should consider and manage for maximum positive impact.

Instructors and Staff

Operating within the learning environment are the T&D staff and instructors. These key individuals interact most directly with internal clients and therefore must be selected for the appropriate individual skills. Obviously, you want them to have skill in the languages used in the

Have you considered the various dimensions and delivery systems in your training function, to help promote a learning climate for all learners?

Physical environment of training facilities ☐

The quality of space and privacy, temperature, noise, ventilation, and comfort levels

Learning resources ☐

Number, quality and availability of staff, training packages, equipment, and breakout rooms

Encouragement to learn ☐

Do you have a vehicle for encouraging employees and staff to generate new ideas, take risks, and experiment?

Rewards ☐

Are your people recognized and rewarded for achieving training outcomes? Are the learners recognized for completing a learning intervention?

Conformity ☐

To what extent are your people expected to conform to norms, rules, regulations, and policies for collective interest rather than to think for themselves?

Technology ☐

Are you paying your employees to complete Web-based courses off-hours just as you would pay them to be in class during regular business hours?

Do you encourage employees to post an "in training" ☐
sign on their office or cubical door so that they may complete on-line learning uninterrupted?

FIGURE 2.6 Managing the Learning Environment

region/market and current technical skill and subject matter knowledge. However, their human relations and political skill is of paramount importance. T&D staff must be client focused, having no agenda except to meet the needs of the client organization. Their primary responsibility is to verify the objectives of the client organization and give them what they need. By asking clarifying questions, creating a clear picture of real needs, considering many alternatives, and suggesting several interventions, the T&D staff adds value to the client organization. Figure 2.7 shows another tool useful in helping the training manager to consider all elements of team management.

At this point, you might want to consider whether external vendors would be appropriate to use in the design and delivery of training or whether you need to build the capability in-house. A yearly developmental conference is one way to keep local unit trainers abreast of the latest in training methods.

Learning Process
Essential to the success of managing a multiple-location system is the process of communicating the organizational philosophy on learning process to the regional/market sites. This does not imply that a one-size-fits all methodology is needed. Indeed, cultural attitudes about training have a profound effect on learning process decisions. In the United States, trainers can successfully practice facilitation skills, encouraging group learning and group process. However, in Asia, Africa, and Europe, the instructor is seen as an authority figure to be revered and respected for his or her knowledge. Different cultural expectations mandate different learning processes.

However, some common practices may need to be part of all T&D offerings. For example, should all of the development interventions in a multiple-location organization

Do you observe that the following building blocks are in place in your training team?	
Clear objectives and goals (based on system's objectives)	☐
Openness in discussing issues	☐
Mutual support and trust among your team members	☐
Cooperation to get results	☐
Sound procedures (based on system's procedures)	☐
Appropriate leadership in setting the direction of the team	☐
Regular reviews to assess the progress of plans and performance	☐
Individual development to maintain competencies in their respective areas	☐
Intergroup relations with other departments	☐

FIGURE 2.7 Managing the Learning Team

incorporate 360-degree feedback—such as thirty-, sixty-, and ninety-day follow-up communications? Should all formal courses use experiences and games, or do some subjects need to be taught using models and reinforcement? The methods employed should involve participants as much as possible and allow them to experience skill development directly. For the most part, action learning and experiential learning meet those requirements as well or better than any other method. For instance, a program designed for a sales team might include more team activities, games, and contests. However, a program designed for engineers might be more structured and oriented toward developing processes and systems. Figure 2.8 provides

When preparing and planning presentations, have you considered the following issues?

Purpose: Why are you saying it?

To communicate information to the audience? ☐

To reinforce a learning point or achieve a learning objective? ☐

To open the topic for discussion with the audience? ☐

Audience: To whom are you saying it?

Who is the audience? ☐

How much do they know about the subject of the presentation? ☐

How large is the audience? ☐

Content: What are you going to say?

Have you summarized the theme of the presentation? ☐

Have you listed and selected the points you want to include? ☐

Have you established the time allocations? ☐

Have you collected supporting information for your presentation? ☐

Form: How are you going to say it?

Have you planned the structure of your presentation? ☐

Have you produced guiding notes for yourself and the audience? ☐

Remember to be positive, precise, and pertinent in your delivery. ☐

Consider the use of appropriate visual and training aids. ☐

FIGURE 2.8 Managing the Learning Process

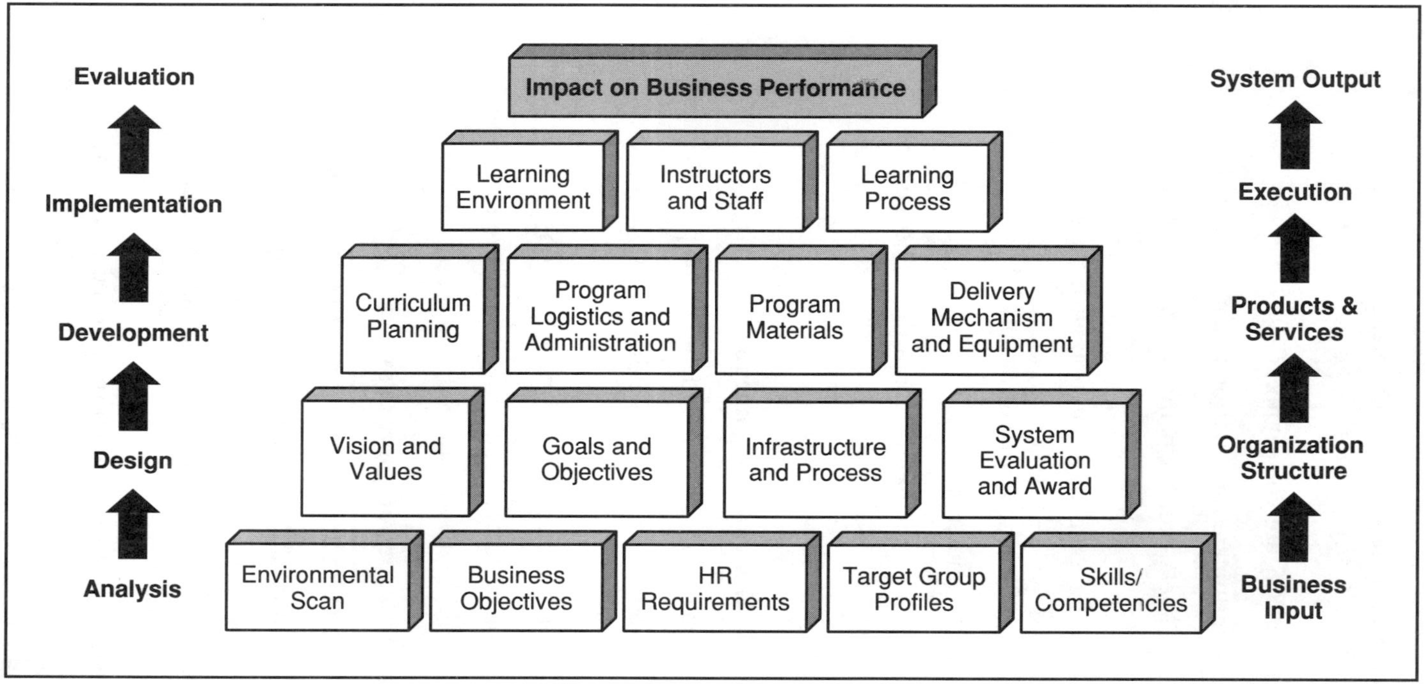

FIGURE 2.9 Multiple-Location System Model: Evaluation/System Output Phase

another checklist of questions to ask in creating the learning environment.

Information from the preceding three inputs suggests how plans should be implemented in terms of process, environment, and staff. While this phase is the most costly, time-consuming, and arguably the most important, it isn't the last phase. This last phase involves evaluating the effects of this phase and those that preceded it.

Phase 5: Evaluation/System Output

It is essential to identify early in the planning process exactly how management will evaluate the effectiveness of the T&D system (Fig. 2.9, top row block). T&D goals should clearly link to business outcomes in client groups. At the local level, employees and functions should also have their goals identified in terms of errors reduced, targets reached, projects completed, developmental activities, formal programs to be delivered, conferences to be held, or audits to be conducted. This helps managers of multiple-location T&D functions to organize and follow performance activities at each location so their budgets can be estimated. By recognizing and acknowledging the attainment of business goals and training objectives and by managing budgets closely, individual locations are able to track their own successes.

CONCLUSION

The steps represented by the simple acronym ADDIE can be used to develop high-level organizations and structures using the very same systematic process thinking for which it was created in the design of simple training sessions. A key assumption involved in using these models is that adequate expertise is available to run the entire system. The more diverse and geographically dispersed your organization is, the more important it is to have a well-defined and carefully managed system. Expert management is a critical factor that allows an organization to organize, define, and measure the effectiveness of a multiple-location T&D system. Control that emerges from adequate expertise is even more important when ventures, franchise arrangements, customers, and suppliers are a part of the system. The more "systemic" the function, the more credibility and impact it has.

USING BUSINESS FUNCTIONS AS A FRAME OF REFERENCE

I like business because it is competitive, because it rewards deeds rather than words. I like business because it compels earnestness and does not permit me to neglect today's task while thinking about tomorrow. I like business because it undertakes to please, not reform; because it is honestly selfish, thereby avoiding hypocrisy and sentimentality. I like business because it promptly penalizes mistakes, shiftlessness and inefficiency, while rewarding well those who give it the best they have in them. Lastly, I like business because each day is a fresh adventure.

R. H. CABELL

Adopting a global position affects all business functions of a company. Finance operations, marketing, human resources, research and development, and legal affairs face new and sometimes daunting challenges. In this chapter, we will look at this very familiar business paradigm and establish how we can use that as a framework for building a multiple-location system for the management of training and development functions. For a system cannot operate in a vacuum but rather must operate within a business ecosystem that renders the services necessary to its survival.

For the core business operations of an enterprise, going global can create new challenges. Finance, for example, may find that the current accounting system requires new programs and processes to satisfy specific tax laws and financial restrictions of the various countries in which the T&D function has responsibilities. The problem might be a total lack of or limited automation, where operations must be able to build new plants, secure equipment, and develop both operational and maintenance systems. Supplier bases may need to be developed. Distribution networks must be established or improved. Sometimes the simple notion of quickly transporting finished goods, or goods in process, can be a problem that promotes great anxiety.

These difficulties represent business issues that T&D must understand and address to provide solutions. This means that T&D must have a comprehensive development system in place to ensure that organization plans, strategies, programs, and operations receive the support they need in far-flung locations. In remote and culturally diverse regions, the T&D function ought to operate as a true business partner, ensuring that what it does is completely aligned with the business strategy of its larger company as well as with the regional and market business units.

The decision to create a training system to integrate multiple locations is based on the idea that it is desirable and possible to link information, knowledge, and actions in all of the company's units around the world into a coherent whole. Technology, especially the Internet, provides channels that make the capture, distribution, and transfer of information much easier. Multiple-location training systems help facilitate a common organizational culture among disparate units in international settings through the examples, content, and metaphors used.

However, companies that operate in large economies, like the United States, have quite complex domestic operations, with plants and subsidiary business units distributed widely across the country. Multiple-location training distribution systems are common in countries like the United States, and they experience many of the same difficulties associated with international distribution systems.

The T&D function in domestic operations has the same goals as international settings: to manage knowledge, to develop the organization's culture, to enhance individual performance, and to strengthen the organization's capability. Thus, although some of the issues may differ, the overall challenge is very much the same for domestic and international multiple-location training distribution systems. As companies around the world face increasing competition, the knowledge of even the best-informed employees has a highly reduced shelf life. On top of that, accelerated business expectations create pressures on hiring practices that require every company with a comprehensive distribution system to have T&D available throughout the system. Such distribution systems must be robust, nimble, and fast but also capable of meeting the diverse needs of different companies, cultures, and lifestyles.

T&D AS A BUSINESS UNIT

Another way to create and administer a multiple-location training system is to think about it as a minicompany, with the same roles and management functions as any other type of organization. Most organizations have the functions of marketing, operations, finance, information systems, human resources and development, legal, and research and development. A fully operational training and development function engages in the same functions as the corporation. That is, the goals of marketing, finance, human resources, and information technology must be used by the T&D function as guidelines or supervised as an outsourced function. The following questions may be helpful in building an adequate infrastructure for the T&D function.

- **Marketing**: How are our T&D services going to be marketed, and who will do it?

- **Finance**: How will our services be paid for, and what financial model will be used? Will T&D be a cost or a profit center?

- **Human resources**: What staff positions and competencies will be needed to do the work? How many people will we need to deliver our goals?

- **Information systems**: What computer hardware/software and other technology will be needed?

- **Research and development:** What new methodologies or delivery technologies (CD-ROM, handheld devices, Internet) should be tested?

- **Engineering/facilities:** What offices, classrooms, and/or laboratories will be needed? Do we rent or build our own?

- **Operations:** How will the work of the department be organized?

Answers to these questions provide baseline data for building the infrastructure. The final infrastructure design depends on the budget. Identifying revenue stream and budget amounts are the most critical elements in building the infrastructure of a multiple-location T&D function; the task is to take each of these management functions and discern the role they perform for the T&D organization. When you have identified the critical elements, the key step is to apply them to the T&D function in terms of how the system would use each of the management functions.

MARKETING

The role marketing plays in most organizations is getting products and services to clients. For T&D this means getting products and services—training sessions, training materials, program design expertise, and facilitation and consulting skills—out to the rest of the organization. Using the four *P*s of marketing, ask yourself several questions to identify the role of marketing. Regarding *products*, what products and services will T&D deliver, and what *price*, if any, should it charge? Regarding *place,* how and where will the products and services be delivered? Should they be marketed centrally or in each business or market? Regarding *promotion*, how do you plan to promote the products? Will you use a newsletter, e-mail, Web page, flyers, calendars, pins, or mouse pads?

You should think like people in marketing, but in terms of T&D products and services. The four *P*s define what products and services will be available, how to charge for them, where they will be delivered (centrally or in various locations), and how to raise their visibility. What image or look should the products have? How will you "brand" the T&D function inside and outside the organization? When you have completed the marketing analysis, move to the next management function and apply it to the T&D system.

OPERATIONS

The operations function covers the actual production and delivery of the products and services of the organization. In using operations as a guide, think about how you are going to work the plan that was developed earlier. First, decide how individuals will be deployed throughout the system so as to complete the work of the T&D function. After that, decide who will do the work. For example, are there enough staff members to carry out most of the development work for the T&D sessions, or will it be necessary to use some outside vendors? The roles and responsibilities of regional or divisional staff, in contrast to the training staff in the markets, should be clearly defined. Identifying the duties of employees at each level alleviates many problems down the road.

Finally, decide what regional or divisional managers of T&D are to do. Limit these intermediate managers to creating plans and keeping in touch with headquarters staff and general managers and senior managers in markets and stores. Additionally, they should lead key strategy sessions and reviews. Try to keep them from delivering programs, even though the sessions may be high profile, because they may get "stuck" leading a regular session when they should be maintaining relations with headquarters or conducting an evaluation of a market. Remember that the task of divisional, regional, and corporate managers is to build systems, not to conduct great training sessions; leave the delivery of training sessions to local training managers and staff.

FINANCE

In developing a financial plan for the T&D function, a large part is simply doing what the finance and accounting personnel do at the corporate level: devise budgets, forecast, and create revenue streams to control costs and enhance cash flow. No, you aren't a finance expert, but you need to think like one! In fact, all you really need to do is take your company's profit and loss statement and translate your own line items onto them. Overall considerations depend on the funding model, whether it is a profit center, a cost center, or a partially funded center. These options will be discussed in detail in Chapter 5. However, a big question concerns how you plan to collect revenues and keep costs down.

The budget should evolve out of the design and delivery schedules. In fact, it is actually possible to identify nearly all of the costs associated with the design, development, and delivery of products and services. Make a list of items and calculate the costs and revenue associated with them. If the delivery involves multiple technology platforms, set aside money for upgrading and replacing equipment. Pay special attention to equipment that may be depreciated. Then add overhead for salaries and bonuses to get a fairly complete picture of income and expenditures. Just as you did for marketing and operations, take each management function and superimpose their activities on the T&D function.

HUMAN RESOURCES

The role that human resource departments play in organizations involves recruiting, hiring, and maintaining personnel in the organization. Thus, the first task is to determine the types of skill sets that are required to perform the work in the T&D function. Some of that information was gathered as part of the business analysis described in Chapter 2. There are usually two choices for locating potential employees: select them externally or find them within the organization. The best people to implement the work of the T&D function should be revealed by the business requirements. For example, some locations have special language requirements or need people with operations experience; those demands will dictate the kind of employees that human resources should hire. In other cases, the preferred employees are individuals who have special backgrounds in human resource development. In the T&D function, specialists in this area are the preferred candidates. The amount of travel that T&D employees are required to do might also dictate who would be most appropriate.

After hiring the best-qualified human resource development professionals, decide how to develop them and keep them enthusiastic about their jobs. Could you make their work more challenging and exciting? Consider giving them new projects to do or an opportunity to work in new areas they have not worked in before, such as engaging in Web-based training, conducting simulations, or working in business operations where they have no previous experience. In each case, make sure you have defined a plan of action for their careers and a development plan to assist them in moving ahead. This way, you have a sustainable proposition for the long-term development of employees in the T&D function.

You should also seek potential candidates—and develop a succession plan—for your replacement. This might seem like a premature strategy, but it is better to begin now than be unprepared later. The other consideration is the development of local training managers and their teams in the markets. Through a market audit, you can discover how knowledgeable and competent managers are in almost all areas of the T&D function. When deficiencies surface, it is a good opportunity to provide mentoring for them. In fact, headquarters, divisional, and regional managers of T&D functions should compile a set of tools that support each step in the T&D process to use in developing local T&D managers and their teams.

MANAGEMENT INFORMATION SYSTEMS

Management information systems (MIS) deals with computer systems that help an organization get and distribute information. In most organizations, MIS includes both hardware and software installation and maintenance. Because of the general boom in the information society and the widespread use of the Internet, the MIS function often helps set the direction of the entire company.

As with the other functions, the highest priority is to create a checklist of MIS concerns. Identify the software and hardware requirements for administering a company-wide, multiple-location T&D system. Make sure that computer systems have direct links to T&D responsibilities. Many vendors can provide helpful solutions to the problem of integrating computer systems with T&D needs so as to use Web-based, computer-based CD-ROMs or digital disks in training. Wherever possible, explore MIS needs with a specialist to maximize employee performance and enhance the connectivity of the multiple-location system. In the future, T&D functions supported by the best electronic systems will be the most efficient and cost-effective.

A training administration and management software program can handle all aspects of registration, task management, certification monitoring, and employee training histories. It should be linked to the human resource information system at headquarters. You may want a software package to design individual training sessions. With such a program, information from each location can be pooled to track and evaluate the progress of employees.

A software vendor that provides the services and could assist the T&D function in acquiring new technology might be contacted. Many available computer programs allow organizations to schedule session locations and times and to assign resources, as well as to list courses, notify participants, and even track a waiting list of potential participants. Many computer programs can track employee-training histories, a requirement of some regulatory agencies. Other important features include tracking all related costs, collecting program fees, and compiling budgets. The programs also track modes of delivery, including CBT, third-party vendors, and distance learning courses.

WHAT INFORMATION WILL YOU NEED TO COLLECT?

When you have chosen a software package, you need to decide on the amount of detail and information you want to manage. There are really only three main levels for which information is required: local, regional, and corporate. Let's look at what you should be collecting at each level:

Local—detailed When reviewing the type of information that the markets are collecting, expect to have a lot more detail at the local level. Detailed information allows the markets to keep tabs on what is happening with their participants and instructors and provides feedback to their designers. Data on who has taken what courses are essential to support human resource development plans. Also, evaluation data at the local level should give the market information it needs to determine how well the transfer of learning is taking place. Tracking the number of training hours completed by each staff person, measured against the goal, also creates a great picture of who has been completing appropriate training. Markets should also be required to capture cost information for their budgets. This detailed information sets up the base from which information is collected at other levels.

Regional or divisional—selective Regional or divisional levels need data on what is going well in the various businesses. Collect information on goals and objectives set for the various markets, including the percentage of sessions completed, percentage of certifications completed, training hours completed, and ratings of training effectiveness. These data should be pooled and analyzed for regions or divisions.

This information should indicate where the markets are having trouble within their specific operations. Information is best obtained on a monthly basis; however, it must be acquired no less than quarterly for regional or divisional levels. This information serves as input for newsletters and reports to senior management. The results of audits and reviews should be part of the information that is reported to upper management. The performance of training professionals at regional and divisional levels should be very high if they expect to improve the overall performance of local markets.

Corporate—filtered Before information is passed on to headquarters, it should be consolidated. Summaries allow corporate officials to get a concise picture of happenings in the field and not get bogged down in the details. Consolidated information indicates more directly who is performing at expected standards. If headquarters does not have a T&D function of its own, then regions and divisions should use their newsletters to tell their own stories.

After a strategy that the staff feels works best for the area is developed, the next step is to send out a survey to determine what is currently being done in the local units and whether they can meet their goals within two years. Two years is a realistic time period for disbursed units to achieve new goals, since budgeting for the various units may not have been done for the current year. This automatically puts them into year 2 of the implementation cycle. However, if simple solutions are being used, goals should be accomplished more quickly. The real problem is usually not money; instead, it is the "different from what I am doing now" syndrome. An effective way to overcome this attitude is to hold a conference with focus group meetings to discuss ways to gain commitment to new ways of doing things.

COMMUNICATION PLAN

The system model described in Chapter 2 does not contain an individual block identified as "communication plan." Nevertheless, a comprehensive, culturally sensitive communication plan is essential in communicating the T&D message to client groups such as senior management, employees, and the overall training community. A good communication plan shapes the image of the function, helps cross learning boundaries, and promotes information sharing. A communication plan should answer the following questions with a particular emphasis on designing a plan that works in a multiple-location system:

- How will we inform client groups and top management about ongoing activities?
- How will we inform T&D staff about company goals, objectives, plans, and directions?
- How will we inform staff about negative, sensitive, and controversial issues?
- How will we encourage staff to participate in a steady two-way flow of information?
- How will we expedite information flow regarding important events and situations?

An effective plan has five essential elements:

1. Each organization should have established communication networks to ensure that information is shared among all personnel. The key is to determine who will be told initially and who each of the succeeding individuals will tell until everyone in the organization is informed. This approach also allows every employee to know whom to contact for information.

2. All official messages should clearly and simply show official authorization. The use of letterhead paper with a special signature is usually a good way to demonstrate that a message is legitimate.

3. Messages should be disseminated so that a supervisor always hears the message before his or her subordinates hear it.

4. If one person in a unit is to be told some information, then all personnel who are equally in need of the information should also be told. Such information should be released soon enough to be useful to the individuals for whom it was intended.

5. As a general rule, information should be provided well in advance of rumors, gossip, and conjectures. This also means that every effort should be made to ensure that accurate, non-distorted messages are available throughout the organization.

Although adhering to these basic guidelines has been found to aid in fostering an effective information distribution system in an organization, research also shows that a primary determinant to messages transmitted, how they are transmitted, and how they are interpreted is the "climate" in which employees work.

COMMUNICATION CLIMATE

Every organization functions with a climate or atmosphere that reflects the attitudes that managers and employees hold toward how the organization is being managed, toward the people working in the organization, and toward how information is handled in the organization. Six characteristics of an effective climate are as follows:

1. **Trust:** Statements and actions sustain confidence and credibility.
2. **Participative decision making:** Employees are consulted on issues of policy relevant to their positions.
3. **Supportiveness:** An atmosphere of frankness and candor exists.
4. **Openness in downward communication:** Employees have access to information about the company, its plans and its leaders, and that relates directly to their immediate jobs.
5. **Listening in upward communication:** Information from subordinates is sufficiently important to warrant action until demonstrated otherwise.
6. **Concern for high-performance goals:** Managers and employees have high aspirations and seek to achieve goals effectively and efficiently.

The Communication Climate Inventory (CCI) is a reliable estimate of the climate of an organization (see the appendix). With a communication plan to achieve these objectives, information flow in the organization will be supportive and working conditions will be optimized.

Cultural Sensitivity

Corporate culture was discussed in Chapter 1, but we wish to highlight here the principle that local employees may have different sensitivities to word usage, content relevance, and cultural norms. In most cases, the "we are different because . . ." syndrome, which is merely a cousin to the "not invented here syndrome," passes if you stick to your game plan. You should be able to get over any initial protest if you remember that one of the roles of the T&D function is to maintain and disseminate the culture of the organization. This theme needs to be reinforced over and over again, especially when employees are part of a corporate captive audience. To maintain the organization's culture, T&D staff must determine what pieces of the organization's culture are most important to reinforce.

By "pieces of culture," we mean the company vision, the management philosophy, operating tenets, and "war" stories. To achieve the culture objective, companies have signed partnership pacts and sponsor major yearly events such as rallies and dinners or meetings that stress "the way we work around here." Some companies post awards and pictures of employees on the reception room walls, and, of course, many companies have informal guidelines that represent a dress code. The important feature of a strong company culture is the extent to which it "carries" throughout the company. For example, a very informal culture may be interpreted and implemented quite differently in Europe and Asia. When all is said and done, culture has to do with how people treat each other. Nevertheless, leaders in the organization ultimately have the greatest influence on the strength of the company's culture.

In a multiple-location system, one of the most important communication strategies is marketing communication. What makes up the elements of this strategy? First, get an identity, a logo, and a name that is synonymous with your organization; they become your "brand name." With these, you can think about promoting the brand through newsletters, a Web site, the course catalogue, binders, bulletins, the training calendars, monthly e-mails, and the needs analysis surveys. Remember that these components of the communication strategy should have the same look and feel. This branding becomes important in establishing an image that should spell professionalism and importance. Always remember that beyond content, which we assume is excellent, impressions count the most.

Organizational Visibility

A communication bonus is derived from enjoying a high level of visibility in the organization. What has been done that people can "see" as evidence of the presence of the training and development function in the area? Outputs should include the following:

- **Yearly schedule**—a calendar of activities for the whole year that targets delivery dates of programs and major events, including conferences and reviews.

- **Catalog**—a document that describes the programs and activities on the calendar. The catalog is a handy marketing tool to explain to others what the T&D function does, when they're going to be done, and where events will be offered.

- **Newsletters**—Some people question the use of newsletters, especially when Web pages are available. They argue that information needed can be put on the Web. However, newsletters are real materials that people can touch and feel, and they can be left in areas or offices where people can "see" them. A Web page is only as good as when it is turned on, and then it is usually serving an audience of one. Newsletters can be handed out to employees as they leave work. Family members also read newsletters.

- **Awards**—Certificates presented to participants at the end of each program, to employees during annual review, to excellent trainers, and to particularly attentive SMEs, reinforce desirable values and attitudes and raise the visibility of the organization as they appear in offices around the organization. They become your icon.

Managers of the T&D function might like to do all the above; however, a more limited strategy that includes three core and two subsidiary elements works just fine. The three core communication elements might be the newsletter, a Web site, and a training calendar. The subsidiary elements could include e-mail and surveys. The question now becomes, Who is the target audience? Is it everybody in the company, just those who have completed certain sessions, or employees at a certain level within the organization? Does that include franchisees? If you are not in the franchise business, targets should probably include customers, suppliers, and vendors.

CONCLUSION

Business functions serve as a frame of reference for developing a multiple-location T&D function. The major business functions—marketing, operations, finance, human resources, and management information systems—supply the resources and function needed by the multiple-location T&D function. As a separate organization within the total system, training and development must incorporate that same paradigm and utilize those business functions in the fulfillment of its function. In such a way, the traditional business paradigm wraps itself around the system to define the external environment while the specific functions of the paradigm enable the system to function.

THE ROLE OF TECHNOLOGY IN THE SYSTEM

We must discard the idea that past routine, past ways of doing things, are probably the best ways. On the contrary, we must assume that there is probably a better way to do almost everything. We must stop assuming that a thing that has never been done before probably cannot be done at all.

DONALD M. NELSON

Many corporations are defining/redefining their technology strategy. What role should T&D play in helping shape its thinking on this issue? In the broadest sense, T&D functions within the arena of knowledge transfer and communication, which are central to the use of technology. More specifically, it is responsible for sharing best practices and implementing on-line learning. Therefore, we will define the lead role it can play in the selection of technology, moving it to the forefront of corporate decision making by demystifying the process and anticipating issues or problems while ensuring that its needs are met. Later, we will look at specific variables to consider before implementing new technology and at thirteen multiple location corporations and how they use technology to manage their operations and educate their workforce.

Many technology options are available for supporting the multiple-location system. The obvious solution may be using an intranet or the Internet to link locations. But before making this assumption, you will want to ask yourself what you are trying to accomplish by using technology and which one(s) are best. The answer to these questions will depend on your technology strategy.

STRATEGIES IN USING TECHNOLOGY

A manager's strategy depends on many variables. What Internet/intranet strategy does the corporation employ, and will that affect T&D plans? Who champions the strategy, and are you in contact with that person? How do the needs of outlying units relate to the needs of headquarters? Should units down the line be managed independently, or should all of the databases be centralized? What do you really need, and how do you find the right tools? Where can technology help in the management of the T&D function?

Technology can help in many places. Imagine yourself as a regional or divisional training manager. You log onto your computer Monday morning, checking the status of last week's training. You look at the forecast numbers versus the actual numbers for training conducted. You click on classroom assessments to see how your trainers performed. You scan a few a pages to see whether the thirty-, sixty-, and ninety-day follow-ups have taken place automatically and whether participants are submitting assignments. As you plan the next trip to visit business units, you check the self-sufficiency scores of participants to see where the business units need help. What commitment to assist them came out of the last action planning session? You look at some key managers' individual development plans to assess how they are progressing. Then you track programs under development to determine whether they are going to meet defined needs. You scroll down and check who has attended the various programs offered on the Web, CBT, CD-ROM, and in the classroom. You check the progress of sessions under development by regional/local teams. For completed programs, you check the status of the translation effort. Finally, you scan through the level 1, 2, and 3 evaluation data to determine what is being applied on the job.

Training technology should be able to help you in all these situations. Your task is to decide what level of sophistication you want, how much you can afford, and how much you are willing to introduce. Selecting the most useful technology begins with asking the right questions:

- What business issue are you trying to solve?
- How much has been or should be budgeted for this project?
- Have the appropriate stakeholders been sold on the project?
- Is there a common personnel or human resource information system (HRIS) that you can leverage?
- How many locations will you need to link?
- How many T&D personnel have access to the Internet on their desktop?
- What information do you require for your system, and why?
- How is information currently captured, and how is it going to be captured?
- Who is responsible for capturing it in each market?

Based on the answers, here are several options to consider. Remember the most sophisticated technology may not always be the right solution. You may have time to grow into a particular solution, or you may need to integrate into an existing system. The goals that drive your technology decisions must be defined before you can meet them. Those technology drivers provide a framework for fitting T&D into the larger organizational technology solution.

TECHNOLOGY DRIVERS

The process of identifying technology drivers and their impact on the organization is a process of asking the right questions of people who have the right answers. One of the strengths that T&D brings to the corporation is the ability to facilitate discussion on many issues. This facilitative skill is needed to move a multifunctional group in the best direction. In creating the strategic plan for using technology, employ these questions and others to clarify the thinking of decision makers and yield a better result for the organization.

1. **Knowledge capture**: How does the organization capture information now? Is the system and outcome adequate? How should it capture and organize newly created information in the future?

2. **Information state**: How much of this information is "static" and can be entered into a database for reference? How much needs to be updated on a daily/hourly basis to yield competitive advantage? Who has the greater interest in doing so? Can some information be on and distributed via CD-ROM rather than occupy space on the Internet/intranet?

3. **Distribution**: How important is it for the entire organization to have access to both static and dynamic information? How will we ensure that the right people know it is there and are using it to improve the business?

4. **Standardization**: How will we ensure that information is updated and correct in all locations? If corporate objectives or training materials change, where and how are they updated? What is the process, and who is responsible?

5. **Speed and time to market**: What information is needed in the market now? What can wait? What impact does centralization versus decentralization have on this question? Who has the resources to keep information updated?

6. **Efficiency**: Is the business process as efficient as we can make it before we automate it? What realized savings or value can we attribute to it? Has someone completed a cost-benefit analysis?

7. **Redundancy**: How much redundancy should we build to ensure that information is backed up, protected, and safe?

8. **Tracking**: How much tracking of documentation do we need? How sophisticated do we need the overarching content management system (CMS) to be, or should we have separate systems with defined sets of information?

9. **Legal**: Considering the information in our system, what legal issues, liabilities, and/or exposure will the company face? Will we provide access to external entities such as vendors, suppliers, franchisees, joint venture partners, or others?

As the facilitator, T&D can raise these questions, among others, and assist in answering them. Participating in the implementation of a company-wide technology solution puts T&D at the forefront of strategic development and showcases a broad understanding of technology and its impact on workforce/learning management. This participation is most effective when the appropriate amount of attention has been paid to political issues and potential problem areas.

CAUTIONS AND CONCERNS

It has been said that if the automobile had followed the same development cycle as the computer, a Rolls-Royce would today cost $100, get a million miles per gallon, and explode once a year, killing everyone inside. In somewhat the same way, if a training director follows a development process better suited to some other function, she or he can get into trouble. One of those high-risk opportunities comes during a technology-related implementation. If you have carefully answered the preceding questions, you will have clarified your thinking about what you want. Now you can help others clarify theirs. You will probably have the opportunity to partner with the information technology (IT) department or whatever group is responsible for the technology solution. It is essential that you not only clarify their thinking on the implementation but also steer them toward a process that works for both organizations. The roles in the process are as follows:

- Business unit—understands the business problem
- T&D—facilitates and asks questions to clarify thinking
- IT—implements a technology-based solution

Having identified the roles, the caution must now be sounded that some organizations are progressive—with some IT departments being active change agents and some not. In some cases, lack of cooperation and challenges can delay the project. This is especially so if an outside vendor or consultant is used. It may be helpful to anticipate these issues and predetermine how to handle them to minimize their impact.

Issue 1: What Happens if Technology Changes?

Technology is going to change. However, we can minimize the impact of changing technology by selecting a solution that is current and operates on a platform that is flexible and accessible to all potential users. The IT function can advise on technology trends and many implementation issues. Do existing applications have the capability to perform the functions desired? Can existing platforms be used to run newly selected applications? What other platforms might integrate seamlessly with current organizational systems? Who can be responsible for integrating the new applications and training users?

Issue 2: Shall We Build or Purchase the Solution?

Because of its knowledge of the organization's business and technological environment, IT can add tremendous value in helping stakeholders understand why things need to be done in a particular way or suggest alternatives. However, unless IT has a track record of actually building customized solutions, you may want to campaign for outsourcing the development of the solution—or purchasing one that has been proven successful in similar organizations. Having selected an application, the question becomes who should implement and integrate the solution—in-house staff or a vendor? Beware the tendency of some IT groups that prefer to build every solution in-house. But unless there is a known expertise there, the building of solutions is best left to proven experts.

Issue 3: Do Participants Share a Common Goal?

An implementation project may have many stakeholders, but they will not all be equally invested or interested in the outcome of the project. An actual case from a vendor's point of view illustrates how disparate goals can affect the implementation of a technology-related project. In this case study, a nationwide chain of convenience stores had a project requiring a technology-based solution. The IT department offered to select the best technology; this was an appropriate role for it to play. However, it failed to deliver on time. A complete revamping of delivery methodology was required to keep the project on track. Here is the story as told by the vendor:

> In addition to our usual consulting services, we produce video programs and multimedia applications. We were asked to produce a video-based training program as part of a larger intervention to help solve a multimillion-dollar problem. Time to market was a critical success factor. Store level staff was the target audience, but there were no VCRs or TVs in the store. So we had a distribution challenge. In a meeting with the IT department, we decided to deliver the program on CD-ROM for playback on an existing computer platform in the stores. IT insisted that we create a "silent" software installer for the QuickTime Media Player—one that needed no end-user involvement to install. Normally, IT would be responsible for this, but we agreed to do it. IT was responsible for equipping all the computers with speakers for audio playback. We each went about our respective tasks and periodically met to test our installer.
>
> A few weeks later, we demonstrated the master CD, our installer, and the video program to our training department client and the IT team. Everything worked flawlessly. As we began discussing a deployment schedule, the IT staff interrupted us to say that they hadn't yet selected which speakers they were going to use and that it would take at least ten weeks to install them in stores after they arrived. This meant we would completely miss our critical rollout

dates for training this key audience. To salvage some of the effort, we had to create a PowerPoint self-study guide and job aid using frame captures from the video. Six months have passed, and the IT department is still evaluating speaker options.

This case study could have involved stakeholders from any of a number of departments. It represents one of many ways that departments with competing priorities, agendas, and action schedules can defeat each other's efforts if they fail to address those issues early in the project.

Issue 4: Do We Have "Not Invented Here" Syndrome?

It sometimes becomes an issue when the point of contact and access to the organization come in through points other than IT. However, many functions will have exposure to software vendors or software solution companies possessing specific technology solutions. In fact, many will have solutions to enterprise-wide problems. The challenge then becomes to give IT enough ownership of the project for them to feel that it has a role in putting the solution together. Otherwise, the old "not invented here" syndrome takes over, and any good ideas presented by others are discredited and vetoed because IT didn't initiate them.

Issue 5: Is Top Management Support Visible?

Every organization wants to deploy their limited resources toward a project that has top-management support. The technology function wants that, too. However, beyond support, IT wants visible recognition—the kind that leads to public accolades for its role in meeting the project goals. Lack of visible top-management support can sap initiative. Competing priorities can subordinate your project to another one. Therefore, it is advisable to garner visible support before you begin.

Some T&D managers, fearing a lengthy approval process, may be tempted to fly their project under radar so that it will not be delayed. Resist this temptation. A stealth project can suffer from rumors, poor information flow, sloppy technical design, and low levels of cooperation from other departments. A better approach is to get approval for general protocols and policies. Adhere to these in undertaking new projects. As long as you operate within these guidelines and follow the protocols, you will have some flexibility. The process of identifying target groups, completed in the analysis/business input phase, should have identified potential sponsors from among those groups that need your services and thus will benefit from the project. If possible, you may want to find a sponsor. However you do it, your IT department and other implementation partners need to know that your project has powerful support and visibility.

TECHNOLOGY-BASED TRAINING IMPLEMENTATION

The T&D function does not have complete control over macrolevel issues affecting corporate-wide technology implementations. It has more control over those issues that primarily affect one of the T&D roles or responsibilities. You will want integrated systems to manage the T&D function. The checklist in Figure 4.1 might be helpful in identifying the specific features of an appropriate system and other variables that affect the technology implementation

Many organizations now employ technological distribution systems, through an intranet or the Internet, to support their business operations wherever they exist in the world. This provides a vital platform for linking employees, suppliers, customers, and licensees into a vital

Type of System
- Training management system
- Learning management system
- Knowledge management system

Hardware
- Intranet-based, server/server network
- Internet-based, server/server network

Types of Training Managed
- On-line only
- Instructor-led only
- Both

Support for Content Applications
- Videoconferencing
- Web-based training
- CD-ROM
- Chat
- Whiteboard
- Streaming video
- Live audio
- Other multimedia

Support for Administrative Applications
- Testing, pre- and postcourse
- Tracking of scores, classes, attendance
- Level 1 and 2 course evaluations
- Multiple levels of administration
- Progress check for students
- Courseware design
- Course prerequisites
- Course registration

Compatibility
- Other management systems already in place
- Other databases used by your company
- Operating system (Windows NT, Windows 98, UNIX)
- Other software to which the client wants to export data

FIGURE 4.1 Checklist for Technology Implementation

Customization
- Courseware
- Management system itself

Contract Issues
- Number of licenses needed
- Availability of system (24 hours/day, 7 days/week, 8–5 Monday–Friday, etc.)
- Levels of service
- Length of service contract (6 months, 1 year, 3 years)
- Availability of technical/field service support (hours of operation
- End user training

Technical Support
- In-house technical support
- Vendor support from management system and/or courseware developer
- Length and availability of free technical support
- Cost of technical support

Installation
- Client or vendor
- Cost

Reliability
- Response time to problems and questions
- Vendor's history of system downtime
- Effectiveness of technical support

Courseware Development—In-house or Outsourced?
- In-house development staff
- In-house development software
- Adequate vendor pool
- Adequate budget for vendor
- Development time for material
- Compatibility of vendor-delivered courses with in-house technology

communication network. Although there are bandwidth and accessibility problems across different countries, with constant improvement in hardware and software, company Web portals are changing the way employees are connected. Later in this chapter, we will share the experiences of several companies to learn how they select technological platforms.

Competence in Internet understanding is essential for global training professionals, whether they reside in markets, regions, or corporate levels. If the organization has a Web portal, the training system model with its building-block format can easily integrate into a centralized T&D Web site. By providing regional and local organizations access to this Web site, you can use the model as a link to tools and additional resources available to support them. If you have done additional research on the Web, the model can direct the user to appropriate sites that reinforce the content discussed. This allows instant access to anyone across different time zones.

Using the model as a resource also facilitates the hiring and training of new regional staff members. The model clearly differentiates between those tasks and roles performed at corporate, regional, and market levels and makes that information available to all. Tools, assessments, and examples of each could also be part of the orientation of new staff. As organizations realize the potential of the Internet, training will truly have its work revolutionized since training is one of the very few functions to be involved across the entire functional spectrum of the organization. With the power of information at everyone's fingertips, this becomes a powerful combination.

How do you achieve the above? Several of the learning and training management systems have extensive reporting capability ranging from cost models to profit and loss statements. One of the major choices you will make is in the selection of a learning management system (LMS) or training management system (TMS). The original tool was the TMS, a computer-based software package that might or might not have been Web-enabled. It tracked courses, attendance, and instructor performance. The newer tool, an LMS (sometimes known as a knowledge management system), organizes, tracks, and delivers training through a central interface over an LAN, intranet, or the Intranet setting. Although the specific functions of an LMS vary based on the vendor, such systems can manage every learning approach typically used in a corporation and offer some or all of the following features:

- Skill competency mapping and skill gap identification
- Integration of on-the-job and instructor-led training
- Learning portfolio maintenance for individual employees
- Manager approval and monitoring of employee training plans
- Training deployment to remote locations
- Classroom scheduling
- Employees linking to Web-based training
- Assessment administration, scoring, and reporting
- Best-practices sharing
- Chat room monitoring, security, and administration

Some products finding acceptance in the market include Click2Learn's Ingenium, KnowledgeSoft's LOIS, Macromedia's Pathware, and Allen Communication's Manager's Edge.

Using these packages to manage training administration is usually more economical than using a manual or nonintegrated computer system, since fewer people are needed to manage the details. These full-service programs allow you to track both traditional and Web-based training for your employees as well as training of external partners, who may need to have accurate records to track certification requirements. The Internet provides the technology needed to offer learning experiences to employees, partners, vendors, and franchisees, which may enable you to spread the costs for generic Web-based program over a larger number of trainees.

WEB-BASED LEARNING

Many studies show little difference in learning accomplishment between classroom training and distance learning. However, employees often complete distance learning faster than classroom training, thereby reducing the length of time needed for training and the cost of paying both trainer and trainee. According to one study, the course compression and potential for a wider audience is chiefly responsible for the production cost advantage of distance learning. The higher fixed cost of Web-based training (license fees for learning platform software, hardware purchase/upgrade) is offset by the reduced operating cost when Web-based training is used to train multiple employees. The companies represented in Table 4.1 have disclosed specific cost savings for using technology-based training instead of classroom-based learning. This does not mean these will directly correlate to your organization. However, you can get a sense of the potential savings these particular organizations have realized.

As with any new endeavor, budgetary considerations arise for the implementation of technology-based training. Potential start-up costs, cost benefits, and cost liabilities are represented in Figure 4.2. Use this tool to guide your thinking about the budget and other financial considerations when implementing technology-based training.

TABLE 4.1   Specific Cost Savings

Company	Savings
KPMG	Web-based training saves the company 70 percent over traditional methods and is developed in a fraction of the time.
Boeing	By training 22,000 managers via satellite, Boeing saved over $9 million dollars in travel expenses. The overall cost per student for one course was $235, about one-half that of traditional delivery.
Dow	In the first three years of using TopClass, Dow expects to save at least $20 million in travel and downtime costs.
GTE	With the help of technology, the training function at GTE Telephone Operations is able to provide training for the entire corporation with less than one-half of its original staff size.
IBM/ semiconductor industry	By standardizing content and delivery through technology-based training, they anticipate savings of hundreds of thousands of dollars due to the drastically reduced number of errors committed during training.

USES OF TECHNOLOGY-BASED TRAINING IN MULTIPLE-LOCATION CORPORATIONS

The changing role of the training professional now includes keeping abreast of advances in technology and delivery mediums. Where do we find information on these trends for the future? The *Masie Newsletter* and *Brandon Hall* newsletter are good places to begin, as are on-line learning and technology conferences. Benchmarking visits to leading companies is another way to obtain targeted information. With this in

Potential Startup Costs
- Training/learning management system purchase
- Technical infrastructure
- Development/purchase of platform
- Development/purchase of content for on-line programs

Potential Cost Benefits
- Reduced travel costs
- Reduced facility costs
- Reduced trainer salary costs
- Reduced losses of downtime
- Flexibility—configurable to individual user's needs
- Easy to distribute and update

Potential Cost Liabilities
- Often longer development time
- Bandwidth restrictions
- Hardware requirements
- Startup costs

FIGURE 4.2   Considerations for Technology-Based Training

mind, we have outlined information on fourteen companies and their training technology choices (Table 4.2). Even though this is not an exhaustive list of training technology, it will give you an idea of the choices these organizations have made to distribute training to their multiple locations. Each uses different forms of technology-based training distribution in addition to traditional classroom training (e.g., satellite, Internet, intranet, or CD–ROM).

Motorola

Motorola University (MU) is one of the largest corporate universities in the world. It has built a vast network of

TABLE 4.2 Uses of Technology in Multiple-Location Companies

Company	CT	WBT	CBT	SAT	VC	Management System	Number of Employees
Motorola	X	X	X	X		Plateau TMS	140,000
Ford Motor Co.	X	X	X	X		Solstra LMS/KMS	400,000
Boeing	X	X	X	X		TrainingServer TMS	190,000
Dow Chemical Co.	X	X	X			TopClass TMS	50,000
GTE	X	X	X			KnowledgeBank KMS *(proprietary)*	114,000
MCI Telephone Co.	X	X		X	X	IT IS TMS *(proprietary)*	77,000
Kinko's	X	X				LiveLink KMS	25,000
Arthur Andersen	X	X	X	X		Ingenium LMS	60,000
						KnowledgeSpace KMS	
Hewlett Packard	X	X	X	X			140,000
IBM	X	X	X				220,000
Rockwell Collins	X	X	X		X	Pinnacle Multimedia LMS	14,000
Bank of Montreal	X	X	X		X		35,000
Buckman Labs	X	X				K'Netix KMKS Ingenium	1,200
Qualcomm	X	X	X			MySource TMS *(proprietary)*	6,000

Key: CT: classroom training
WBT: Web-based training (asynchronous)
CBT: computer-based training (non-Web-based—e.g., CD-ROM, virtual reality, etc.)
SAT: live satellite broadcast
VC: virtual classroom (live via Internet/intranet)

campuses in twenty-three countries. Historically, to fulfill Motorola's requirement of forty hours of training each year, employees traveled hundreds and thousands of miles to learning campuses, frequently to the main campus outside Chicago. MU chose the "best and brightest" instructors and trained them for three to six months before they began teaching (Greenberg, 1998, p. 37).

Motorola still places high value on learning, and each year tens of thousands of employees flock to MU learning centers. However, in recent years the company has begun to incorporate more technology into its training program, allowing some training to occur away from the main campuses. By 2001, Motorola will require 35 percent of all its training to be done online. In 2002, the requirement will rise to 50 percent (Dobbs, 2000, p. 55). The College of Learning Technologies (CLT), a division of MU, is helping the university explore its options for technology-based training. Charged with finding the best ways to use technology for training, it has focused on several training areas.

MU's Learning Forum enables employees to take courses from their offices on the company intranet. This option mainly serves IT professionals and engineers in the United States, along with some in Asia and Europe. It also offers other courses such as software application ("Motorola University's Learning," p. 9). MU uses on-line course material from an array of vendors such as Netg ("On-Line Learning," p. 1). Other Web-based courses are available to all employees via the Internet through LearnShare. To ensure that technology and equipment are available to the dispersed workforce, MU maintains learning labs at sites around the world. Using media, including CD-ROM, video, and the Web, students can study an array of topics ranging from stress reduction to laser safety training.

LEARNSHARE

LearnShare is a consortium of thirteen noncompeting companies and three universities that share courseware on cross-company issues such as diversity training. They also use their combined purchasing power to receive group discounts from courseware vendors and work together to develop new material, which is then owned by LearnShare. At least 25 percent of the available materials is on-line, while the rest can be ordered in paper or CD-ROM versions (LearnShare 2).

LearnShare

With help from Carnegie Mellon University, Motorola implemented just-in-time lecture (JITL) learning. JITL is a low-cost training medium that Motorola implemented. Combining CD-ROM multimedia capability with the flexibility of the Web, a JITL usually includes an hour of lecture on digitized video, PowerPoint material, a navigation index, and frequently asked questions. Videoconferences allow instructors to reach a wider audience than they could otherwise in the classroom, and it also eliminates travel costs. Combining 3-D models, audio, text, and video, virtual reality gives employees the chance to experiment with realistic virtual "equipment" without the risk of damage to the equipment (Rucker, 1999, pp. 5–6). In December 1999, Motorola began using the Plateau learning management system from Plateau Systems to manage its training, which allows Motorola employees worldwide to view their training options and progress and register for classes ("Motorola University Implements").

Ford Motor Company

Ford Motor Company uses a variety of training methods to meet the needs of its various departments and divisions. One of the best known is the FORDSTAR satellite system, used with its 6,800 North American dealerships ("Filling the Dealer," 1997, p. A26). FORDSTAR is one of the most extensive real-time video training networks in the world. The system combines very small aperture terminal (VSAT) satellite technology from Hughes Network Systems with interactive distance learning equipment from One Touch Systems, Inc. This combination enables one-way video and two-way audio transmission; the students can see, hear, and converse with each other. Ford uses the $100 million system to train all personnel at its dealerships, from mechanics to salespeople to administrators. Topics covered via satellite include time-sensitive material such as product recalls, marketing campaigns, new-model introductions, technical information, and general policies. Before FORDSTAR, training had been difficult for Ford because one-third of its dealerships are located over one hundred miles away from the nearest regional training site. In light of the success of its satellite system, Ford is now expanding to Europe and Australia. Using FORDSTAR and CD-ROM courseware, Ford has moved 92 percent of its dealership training from the classroom to technology based (Careless, 1998).

To train other personnel, Ford relies on a combination of media. For its engineers and many of its other employees around the world, the Ford Design Institute (FDI) is implementing Solstra, a learning management system developed by Britain's Futuremedia and British Telecommunications ("Ford Motor Company," 2000). Solstra, used to manage training for FDI employees in the United States, the United Kingdom, Germany, and Australia, gives employees access to an intranet-based training system and allows

Ford to keep all training information consistent and easily updated. Futuremedia also collaborates with Ford on multimedia courseware. In 1998, it developed an interactive CD-ROM training course for Ford's Global Paint Engineering Division. The course uses digitized video of instructors and comes in several languages. To create the different versions, Futuremedia used subject matter experts from various countries to ensure that the language was localized ("BT and Futuremedia," 1998).

Ford's purchasing department also uses an intranet to manage its training. The system allows on-line course selection and registration, which simplifies the registration process. Switching to the intranet format has made management of the training program more efficient and up-to-date (Ciancarelli, 1998, p. S25). Nevertheless, not all of Ford's training has gone high-tech; some still requires travel. For instance, when Lincoln launched the Lincoln LS in 1999, Lincoln Mercury dealers gathered in San Francisco to prepare for the event (Krebs, 1999, p. 48).

Boeing Aircraft Company

Boeing's innovative Quality through Training Program (QTTP), a career resource and training initiative, has brought the company acclaim and higher productivity. Boeing and the International Association of Machinists (IAM) worked together to develop the program. Through this program, Boeing employees who are members of IAM may receive classroom instruction, utilize a variety of video- and computer-based courseware, and benefit from career and personal development counseling. QTTP can also arrange retraining to help laid-off workers find other jobs within the company. As another training option, all unionized, full-time workers can qualify for unlimited tuition and fees at accredited colleges or universities ("Melanie Brisbane," 2000). The new Career Explorer Web lets workers research job requirements for other positions in the company. Then they determine which additional skills they need and register for the appropriate courses on-line (Barron, 1999).

The program also utilizes satellite technology to train its employees. By using a digital satellite broadcast, instead of the more traditional training conferences, Boeing recently saved at least $9 million in travel costs alone. The company needed to teach strategic planning skills to twenty-two thousand of its managers. Working with Digital Xpress, a satellite communications company, Boeing developed a system that would allow direct video broadcast to sites in the United States, Japan, Australia, and Western Europe. The course included the video broadcast, a site facilitator, audio interaction with course instructors, and off-air activities such as workbooks and other tools on a Web site. In addition to the money saved, knowledge retention rates were impressive and total delivery time for the course shrunk from two years to eight months ("Boeing Takes Care," 2000; "The Boeing Company," 2000). Boeing also uses RealNetworks' RealPlayer to stream video material, such as an address from CEO Phil Condit, across its intranet. Before using RealPlayer, Boeing spent a significant amount of money to duplicate and ship training videos and other material to its employees ("Boeing Deploys," 1997).

Boeing also uses the TrainingServer training management system from Syscom, Inc. Before TrainingServer, Boeing used more than twenty-five separate TMSs and hundreds of informal tracking systems. Frustrated by the inefficiency of the old system, Boeing purchased a commercial off-the-shelf system instead of developing one in-house. By accessing the system through the company intranet, employees can search and register for courses. TrainingServer has saved the company money, administration time, and paper ("First in Flight," 1998).

Dow Chemical Company

With its goal of moving 80 percent of all classroom training on-line by 2001, Dow is a leader in Web-based training. To facilitate the transition from classroom to the Web, Dow bought the TopClass training management system from WBT Systems of Dublin, Ireland. TopClass organizes and feeds course material over Dow's on-line university, learn@dow.now, provides assistance to help Dow's trainers design Web-based courses, and tracks individual training progress (Hanner, 1999, p. 12; Briody, 1999).

In the first nine months of using TopClass, Dow developed thirty-one on-line courses. More than 25 percent of its employees completed at least one course on-line. Two main issues hinder their switch to Web-based training. First, although Dow has recently invested millions of dollars on its computer network, some employees still use older computers that cannot run Web-based applications well (Schaaf, 1999, p. ET16). Second, some employees, particularly those over forty, have difficulty adjusting to the technology-based format (Briody, 1999).

Web-based training allows Dow to simplify its training program and save millions of dollars as well. Instead of underwriting experts and updates of training materials, Dow now posts its training on the intranet for all of its 121 locations to access. The initial return on investment (ROI) estimate was seventeen months, but the conversion is proceeding ahead of schedule, and Dow could see an ROI even sooner. Over the first three years of the program, the company expects to save $20 million in travel time and other training costs (Hanner, 1999, p. 12).

General Telephone and Electronics (GTE)

GTE is a global telecommunications company with several divisions and departments, all of which use a variety of training methods. GTE currently operates under a

"50/50 rule" that requires half of all newly developed training to be technology based (Rayl, 1998, p. 37). Its proprietary Virtual University provides media-rich Web-based training, Internet links to tools, and a training management system. A searchable training database called BASELINE provides GTE course developers with materials. Other self-paced materials rest on CD-ROMs. One WBT course includes a multibranch role-playing module that recreates a sales environment. Although most users of the Virtual University are connected to a company LAN, the developers also included alternate routes through the content for those users with low bandwidth. To manage knowledge throughout the company, GTE uses its internally developed Knowledge Bank. To train its employees on its new Assignment, Activation, and Inventory System (AAIS), GTE uses Web-based courseware developed by click2learn.com, formerly known as Asymmetric Learning Systems ("GTE Selects Asymmetric," 2000). GTE Learning Systems uses a balanced approach that blends classroom training, electronic training, and mentoring. Mentors bridge the gap between the classroom and technology. They schedule meetings with experts, guide the trainee through classes, assign homework, and answer any questions that arise.

MCI WorldCom

Taking advantage of its advanced computer network, telecommunications giant MCI employs a variety of methods for training employees, including distance learning, artificial intelligence, and the Career Enhancement University (CEU), a technical training organization. Its main campus is at the company's headquarters in Richardson, Texas. Satellite broadcasts, intranet training, and classroom training take place in the facility, but it engages employees worldwide. CEU is linked to MCI's training database, the Integrated Training Information System (IT IS), which organizes course registration, tracks employee training, and lets employees evaluate courses (Fryer, 1998, p. 18).

Live satellite broadcast courses are similar to traditional classroom courses except that the class can occur in multiple locations simultaneously. MCI manages its satellite courses through TrainingServer, the same system Boeing uses. MCI runs the interactive aspects of the courses in part through the One-Touch Systems IDL broadcast toolkit, which transmits students' question responses and other information back to the instructor (Stoerp, 2000).

Another distance learning tool is powered by LearnLinc software. LearnLinc supports and integrates a variety of instructional media, including audio- and videoconferencing, electronic "whiteboard," and Web-based courseware ("LearnLinc 4.0 Raises," 1999). The students at each site can use chat software to communicate with one another and look up information online (Fryer, 1998, p. 18). Students can also submit questions to teaching assistants and receive answers as soon as they respond (Mateyaschuk, 1999). MCI uses these classrooms to train its network technicians at hundreds of sites (Fryer, 1998, p.18). LearnLinc operates either over the MCI intranet or the Internet, allowing employees to view courses at client sites as well as from their own offices (Mateyaschuk, 1999).

MCI's Virtual Courseware, another proprietary intranet application, uses pictures, video clips, and an artificial intelligence "instructor" to teach technicians to install a network. Options in the modules include a general presentation and a step-by-step walk-through of the procedures. The "On-Site Tour" uses network monitoring software to give new-hire technicians real-time video of network switching hardware. And the Web Forum, a physical IT conference, has a Web component that allows IT staff from throughout the company to "sit in" on the conference and interact with the conference participants through chat software (Fryer, 1998, p. 18).

Kinko's

Kinko's, a full-service printing company, puts all its employees through a stringent training program. New hires report to one of Kinko's regional training sites for a five-day orientation. There they learn how to operate Kinko's printing equipment and work with customers (Duff, 2000). Once new employees return to their work sites, they can use another training resource: Kinko's Online University. Developed by LeadingWay, the intranet-based university enables employees to retrieve product information quickly and easily while on the job. It also offers training courses, including five-minute modules on topics such as sales and software applications. Kinko's employees complete "a whole battery of classes" that enable them not just to make copies but also to converse intelligently with their customers and offer suggestions. Kinko's manages its knowledge enterprise-wide with the Livelink KMS from Open Text Corporation. Livelink, like the Online University, runs over Kinko's intranet.

Arthur Andersen Consulting Company

Arthur Andersen, a global professional services company, varies its training according to subject matter. For most soft-skills training, employees meet at classrooms or conferences at its local offices, its regional training sites, or its main training center in St. Charles, Illinois. For example, in 1999 one American instructor delivered a two-month "immersion" course in business English skills to several of the company's overseas consultants (Kiser, 1999a).

For much of its other training, the company uses technology-based media. The Arthur Andersen Virtual Learning Network (AAVLN) is an intranet-based training system that went on-line in 1999. Powered and managed by the Ingenium LMS from click2learn.com, the AAVLN offers a variety of on-line courses in technical subjects such as finance, tax law, information technology, management, and marketing. For Arthur Andersen, intranet-based training is effective for teaching many basic skills in these subjects. After the on-line training, employees may move on to instructor-based training for further study. Ingenium also tracks the company's classroom-based training. Arthur Andersen manages its enterprise-wide knowledge through its proprietary KnowledgeSpace KMS, which outside users can subscribe to as well. For satellite communications in North America, Arthur Andersen uses technology from DigitalXpress, through which it shares video materials and multimedia services with its employees and also trains them through video broadcasts.

Hewlett-Packard

For a time, Hewlett-Packard (HP) used a satellite broadcast system to deliver product demonstrations to its employees. This system was only partially effective because only 20 percent of the company could travel to downlink sites. To solve this problem, HP developed a low-cost alternative, called DeskTV+, that can train most of its employees around the world. By combining recorded video, audio, and Web-based material, DeskTV+ transmits the training material effectively, cheaply, and on demand over HP's intranet.

To produce a DeskTV+ module, HP technician's record live training presentations, digitize the video, and publish it on the Web. If necessary, they also design a Web site, test questions, or other materials to accompany the video. Like other Web-based materials, DeskTV+ modules are updateable as needed. Their production cost is much lower than CD-ROM material—about $0.50 per user versus $80 (Martinez, 1998, p. 42).

DeskTV+ is not HP's only training method; it is simply one option that HP trainers use to supplement their other methods. For example, along with Web-based training, HP also uses Microsoft NetMeeting, a videoconferencing program that combines live video, live audio, and PowerPoint slides. Unlike DeskTV+, NetMeeting is interactive, but it can only accommodate twenty-five users at a time (Pemberton & Pack, 1999, p. 33).

International Business Machines (IBM)

Like many large companies, IBM no longer relies exclusively on classroom training. Each year, up to fifteen thousand employees still go to the IBM learning campuses, but increasingly they use technology-based methods. These include interactive television, computer-based training, and Learning Space, an asynchronous Web-based system. In Learning Space, the course instructor sets the assignments and content and the students work in accordance with their own schedules (Solomon, 1999, p. 67).

One particularly helpful approach is IBM's virtual reality (VR) program for its semiconductor factory employees. Semiconductor assembly is a very precise process in which a simple mistake can ruin $100,000 worth of chips. Previous training methods—classroom and on-the-job—produced error rates as high as 25 percent. IBM purchased VR software from Modis Training Technologies, Inc., to simulate the manufacturing process and give trainees a chance to practice without putting chips or equipment at risk. Once the VR training is completed, trainees move on to on-the-job training. With this software, the training process takes only half the time and produces only a small fraction of the errors. It also saves the considerable cost of flying workers into training centers from other sites. The simulator can run over the IBM intranet (Greengard, 1998, p. 72).

Rockwell Collins

Rockwell Collins is a leading manufacturer of aviation equipment with fourteen thousand employees. In years past, the company relied mainly on classroom-based training. But in 1999, it began shifting to more technology-based training, including Web-based training, CD-ROM courses delivered via learning labs, and live training via virtual classrooms. Its goal is to have 70 percent of its training switched to an electronic format by 2003. In the process, it expects to offer 40 percent more courses and save at least $14 million.

Cliff Purington, manager of learning and development for Rockwell Collins, joined the company in 1998 with the goal of streamlining its training program. First, he studied the company's current practices and realized that classroom training alone could not fulfill all of Rockwell's training needs. Over one-quarter of all students registered for classes did not attend, often because of other work commitments. Most employees preferred to learn at their own pace outside a classroom environment. In light of this information, Purington's team called for the company to convert most of its training to electronic media. To implement this plan, Rockwell Collins is making several changes in its training structure. Learning councils in each business unit have been created to determine future training needs. In addition, Rockwell belongs to an industry-training co-op that shares computer-based courses over an extranet.

Bank of Montreal (BMO)

The Bank of Montreal (BMO) is another institution that places high value on learning. In 1994, it opened its $50 million Institute for Learning. Its purpose is to help all thirty-five thousand BMO employees develop into proactive, customer-oriented "idea people." It includes twelve high-tech classrooms, a high-tech resources center, eight role-play rooms, and a cafeteria to encourage discussion among employees. In 1995, BMO began giving each employee five full days of education each year. Over 25 percent of all training occurs at the Institute (Flynn, 1997, p. 33). To promote team mentality, it brings in and trains 250 employees from throughout the company each week (Greenberg, 1998, p. 37). Each staff member at the Institute for Learning serves in one of three ways. *Relationship managers* meet with BMO's business units, evaluate their strengths and weaknesses, and decide which learning areas would be most helpful. *Subject matter experts* serve as faculty. *Learning managers* decide the best methods of learning for each person or business unit (Flynn, 1997, p. 33).

In addition to the institute, BMO provides several other options for employee training. Much of the company's instruction occurs near or at the employee's work site or through distance learning, such as on-line help programs and electronic classrooms. In addition, its tuition reimbursement plan pays for college courses such as those taught at the residential MBA program that BMO cofounded with a Canadian university (Flynn, 1997, p. 33).

Buckman Laboratories

Buckman Labs, a manufacturer of specialty industrial chemicals, employs 1,200 people in eighty countries around the world. Like most global companies, it routinely sent instructors to field locations even though it was costly, time-consuming, and ineffective. In an effort to eliminate these problems, Buckman Labs established the Bulab Learning Center, an intranet delivery system for training courseware. The center offers a variety of content, from technical- and business-related courses to material from non-Buckman on-line universities. Employees can access the center from home, during lunch, or even during down-time at work. To be sure, not all of the training offered by Buckman is appropriate for a computer-based format. But the center has made training much more efficient and cost-effective by using the Ingenium LMS to manage its training enterprise-wide.

Another feature of Buckman Labs is its proprietary knowledge management system, K'Netix. One of the most respected systems of its kind in the industry, K'Netix allows Buckman employees around the world to exchange ideas, ask questions, and receive quick answers through the company intranet. In one case, a sales associate closed a multi-million-dollar order because of the technical information provided by Buckman subject-matter experts just hours after the information request (Chaudron, 1998, p. S12).

Qualcomm

Qualcomm is a leader in the telecommunications industry. In accordance with its strong commitment to continual learning, it offers a broad array of training courses, includ-ing more than 250 on-line modules. Available classes fall into four categories: (1) technical courses on their Code Division Multiple Access (CDMA) technology for digital wireless communication, (2) computer training and engi-neering, (3) manufacturing, and (4) professional and man-agement development. Many of these courses are available in both classroom and on-line formats. Increasingly, employees are accessing courses on-line from their homes and hotel rooms instead of arranging their days around an instructor's schedule.

To manage the training program for its six thousand employees, Qualcomm uses learning specialists who study the needs of every business unit and help arrange new courses. Leaders in each unit determine mandatory courses with others being optional. Qualcomm complements its training program with a career management system called MySource. Through it, employees can access their records, consider their skills and accomplishments, register for courses, and see requirements for other positions. The MySource system is linked to Qualcomm's PeopleSoft ERP, which allows supervisors and other administrators to review an employee's work history for evaluations and promotions (Greengard, 2000, pp. 88–90).

CONCLUSION

In Chapter 3 we discussed the essential role of classic business processes as they enable the traditional training function to operate. In much the same way, technology plays a vital role as it empowers the multiple-location system to operate by enabling communication, standardization of processes, and evaluation procedures. Technology is needed to unify the training hierarchy, from unit to corporate levels. In addition, technology is increasingly used by T&D functions as a training tool, expanding media choices beyond the traditional classroom and video. Thus, the need for technology permeates various aspects of the T&D operation while differing only in its application.

CHAPTER 5

MANAGING MULTIPLE-LOCATION SYSTEMS THROUGH REGIONAL CENTERS

The CEO of one state department of agriculture, for example, had found that even regional structures were too large, too amorphous, and had moved towards smaller, autonomous district units. His metaphor said everything: I don't run a ship: I run a flotilla! The problem with such chunking is that it can lead to decoupling. Top managers throughout the West were beginning to face the same persistent problem: what do you do after the consultant has been through your organization, chopped away at the corporate headquarters and flattened the hierarchy?
How do you get efficiencies and synergy now?

DAVID LIMERICK AND BERT CUNNINGTON

In general, regions are created around the markets the company serves, with regional staff given authority and responsibility over activities that require serving their local markets. In this chapter we will explore specific considerations of regional T&D management and look at some tools that facilitate various aspects of the operation. The management of regional operations is unique in the world of training, from reporting relationships through structure and staffing. What are the important questions to ask yourself before deciding whether to build a regional center? How can you raise revenues? What are the five steps to follow in developing your staff? These are important issues that affect the operational performance of the regional center and will be considered in detail in the chapter.

Regions contain their own functional departments—such as purchasing, engineering, manufacturing, marketing, and training and development—and receive their authority from corporate managers. As a rule, corporations give regions extensive autonomy to pursue regional goals but monitor how well those goals have been achieved. As far as training and development is concerned, a director supervises the regional T&D staff, who are responsible for the design, production, and delivery of regionwide programs. The relationship between corporate and regional T&D structures is portrayed in Figure 5.1. The region can also have staff members who are responsible for specific functions of the ADDIE process, such as design and delivery of training. The main difference between the work of the regional and market T&D managers is the regional manager's responsibility to aid corporate training and development to establish a consistent process, uphold standards, build company culture, and provide consulting and change management expertise for the business units across the entire region.

CORPORATE AND REGIONAL T&D RELATIONSHIPS

Each business unit within a market has its own training managers and coordinators who serve as the source of training information for the market, business unit, and company stores. Market training managers serve as the link to the region and are responsible for running the local training function for the local business. Training coordi-

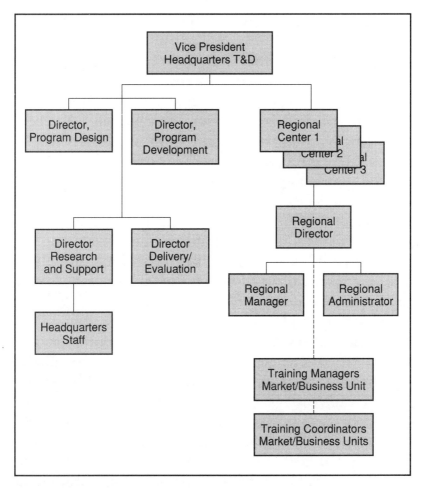

FIGURE 5.1 Corporate and Regional Relationships

nators serve as liaisons between the front-line staff and the market T&D function.

The success of the regional T&D structure depends mostly on the capability and expertise of the regional director and the new T&D teams. Considering all other issues, the capability and expertise of people leading the training function should determine the scope of the center and how much work they can handle. To make the regional director and corporate staff more effective, they must guide the managers and coordinators of markets as well as they can.

Periodically directors are brought back to headquarters for periodic meetings with corporate training to ensure that the broader goals of the company, rather than the more limited goals of the region, are achieved. Mintzberg (1993) argues that the regional form works best with a bureaucratic structure because "the only way that headquarters can retain control yet protect [regional] autonomy is by after-the-fact monitoring of [regional] performance" (p. 219). Although regions might be loosely coupled systems in relationship to one another and the corporation, they are tightly coupled within themselves. This allows the regional director to impose performance measures on units within the region.

Limerick and Cunnington (1993) have argued for an organizational system that resembles "strategic alliances" and "networks" and capitalizes on "collaborative individualism." Loosely coupled network systems allow structures to evolve to meet changing conditions, which places commitment to the issue, mission, and vision at the core employee's concerns rather than allegiance to the organization itself. Each individual becomes a "You, Inc." in which workers form an alliance with the organization, in contrast to being owned by it.

Networking and collaboratively individualistic workers have fostered a new category of worker—the "gold-collar" worker—rather than the blue- or white-collar (Kelley, 1985). Gold-collar workers are emancipated from bureaucratic drudgery and require challenging and imaginative problems to solve and goals to achieve. They are empowered by knowledge and driven by their own values, so as to work interdependently and collaboratively with others while maintaining their own individualism and freedom. The structure that seems most compatible with collaborative individualism and networking alliances has been portrayed as a cluster of circles. Figure 5.2 shows a central entity surrounded by clusters of loosely coupled configurations held together by commitments rather than by authority chains.

Circle clusters represent regional structures better than a straight hierarchy, since they have many of the characteristics of loosely coupled configurations. However, within each circle, it may be essential to have firm hierarchical relations.

INTERNAL STRUCTURE OF THE REGIONAL T&D FUNCTION

The issue to address now is how a regional T&D center ought to be organized internally. If the regional T&D center reports to corporate human resources, as suggested in Figure 5.1, its internal structure might be different from what it would be if it reported to the operations function. This is because structure revolves around the kind of work the function is assigned to do. If T&D is concerned

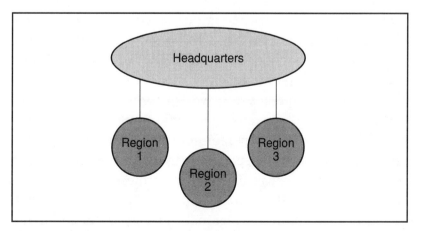

FIGURE 5.2 Regional Circle Cluster Structure

mostly with technical or operations training, the structure of the T&D function is different than if it focused primarily on management development, and it would be different from either of those if it had responsibility for both. Here we're assuming that the regional T&D staff has the responsibility for and skills to do both technical operations management training, making it a fully integrated and complete training unit.

When thinking about the size of a current and future regional T&D center, all the major elements of ADDIE must be taken into account. If the regional center is staffed with only two people, due to its role or budget, the regional manager must define its output very carefully. Regional travel and training schedules are usually heavy, leaving little free time to be creative, plan for the future, and deal with ad hoc requests.

As has been pointed out, regional design and development can be carried out at corporate headquarters. In those cases, very little autonomy is given to the regions. In other instances, the corporate staff design the template and the regions fill in the blanks as needed. In both instances, the need for design staff at the regional level is lessened and the task becomes one of launching projects and conducting train-the-trainer sessions. A two-person regional training team has a reasonable chance of being successful and having a positive impact only when design occurs at the corporate level.

From a corporate perspective, it is important not only to add value to the local customer chain but also to develop the capability of T&D personnel throughout a region. To facilitate that goal, corporate might want to strengthen regional training capabilities with a professional train-the-trainer program. It might also provide a handbook with guidelines for building a regional training center and make available the assessment instrument from Chapter 6 to assess the health of the market training units. That way, the regional training center comes armed with the tools to enhance the quality of market training units.

SELECTION OF REGIONAL STAFF FOR MULTIPLE-LOCATION MANAGEMENT

Managing a multiple-location training and development system requires individuals who have a unique flexibility and can sort out information and correct networking difficulties. They must also be able to manage in situations where there are both detailed corporate guidelines and a great deal of administrative autonomy.

Issue 1: Sizing for Current and Future Needs

When thinking about the size of the current and/or future regional training center, a review of the major elements of ADDIE provides some guidelines. This should lead you to answer questions that reveal what you feel is the regional capability at present and what you should do to build future capability. A number of specific questions should be answered to help think through this issue: How large is the current or proposed regional function? Is a limited budget a stumbling block to an effective operation? How much development work is required versus how many existing programs must be delivered? Does the current regional director have the ability to handle both management and technical training? Does the regional center director possess adequate influence skills to work with senior management? The incumbent regional training director should answer these questions. When in doubt, try to provide an explanation for your answers so that the assumptions you are operating on are made clear. If the question appears to challenge your personal capabilities, the best approach is to become introspective and honestly decide how your personal abilities match the requirements. Continue to seek development in the areas that are most essential to the regional function in the short run, then focus on any longer-term or corporate shifts.

Issue 2: Market or Business Unit Structure

You should answer a number of questions before the previous questions are even posed. These questions should help you think through this issue for your specific company and not be caught off guard. What are the expected demands of the business on the regional center? How will operations and human resources use the regional center? Is there an existing training curriculum that needs to be delivered? Does a training curriculum or learning map have to be developed? What levels within the organization does the training professional have to work with to get the job done? What abilities does the staff need to do the job?

How to Structure the Regional T&D Center

"Structure follows strategy" is a phrase with which we are all familiar. Business schools use this principle to guide their thinking about structure, and it is equally appropriate for examining the structure of a regional T&D function. If the various market managers have given you their requirements and you have defined what you're going to do, then the principle tends to be applicable. However, from a regional T&D perspective, the principle could be stated more accurately as "Structure depends on the breadth and depth of responsibility undertaken by the function."

The next logical step is to determine who should be hired to fill each role. The task becomes more or less difficult depending on the competencies required of the regional team and the internal talent you have to fill those requirements. In many cases, regional staff should have consulting and language capabilities over and above the basic skills for designing, developing, and delivering training programs, depending on which geographic region they are covering. In most cases, the regional staff should decide whether applicants have the technical backgrounds in training and development, as well as the interpersonal and language capabilities, to do the job.

Another staffing consideration involves planning for your own succession. Although this might seem premature, now is the time to prepare others to take on another assignment when you decide to move on. Failure to make these plans as part of initial staffing has often been an Achilles' heel and leads to the failure of many regional functions. In summary, the main issues in staffing concern strategy, interpersonal and technical skills, language facility, and succession planning. Usually at least three possible scenarios affect hiring decisions.

Scenario 1 If training and development is to handle only technical training, then the regional center should be structured around the types of outputs produced and delivered. If this is your region's scenario, you should hire regional staff members who have the required technical background. In many cases, you will need to hire individuals from within the organization. On the other hand, outside hires might be necessary because of the lack of availability of internal resources and to enhance credibility of the training staff within the region.

If you are using internal technical experts, assess their training design and consulting skills by using the model in Chapter 2 as a guide. Specifically, review the model and evaluate their experience with the activities listed in each relevant box. This gives you an indication of the skills required to do the job.

To illustrate this point, Steve explains, "I hired a technical expert, who was considered a rare catch in the organization, into the training function. When he was assigned to assist a client during the first two weeks, they loved him because he was uncovering some of their technical problems and providing solutions. By week 3, he loved his work so much that he became serious about really pointing out weaknesses in the organization and identifying specific individuals as the root causes. At that point, no one appreciated his abilities. By week 4, they did not want to see him again. He was reassigned to another client and received a significant wake-up call on the way he introduced and communicated performance improvement ideas."

As you know, the softer side of the job, or the emotional quotient (EQ), is critical in ensuring that the regional staffs get along with the various business units. Be sure to consider a person's interpersonal skills during the interview stage. If you are hiring people outside the company, a thorough orientation to the company, a unit, and the T&D center is critical, as they are often only accustomed to their previous organization's culture and operations.

Scenario 2 If the T&D function is assigned to handle management development activities, it should be structured around types of development activities. In this scenario, new regional staff must have experience in designing and delivering supervisory, management, and executive development programs. Naturally, if the corporate T&D function provides the design of programs, delivery and facilitation skills become more important. If the regional staff have to build their own programs, individuals with balanced design and delivery skills should be selected.

Staffing might seem easy, but it is not. This is because few people naturally possess design and delivery skills, and those who do are often not available. Seeking out, screening, and selecting individuals who can respond to specific needs is often beyond the reach of untrained human resources personnel. The process is complicated by the demands of working with multiple business units and their individual priorities across the region. The ability to adjust styles of interaction to various situations is also an important skill—but also rare in some regions and countries. The key skills in management development are designing and delivering management content to a cross section of experienced managers. In many cases, management development activities at the regional level are deployed to all business units.

Having a regional team with strong facilitation skills is critical, since you will usually be asked to help develop skills that complement the specific programs presented. For example, the regional staff might facilitate strategy sessions to define processes for business units within markets. When you facilitate these activities, you build useful relationships with key leaders.

Scenario 3 If the T&D function is assigned to handle both technical training and management development, it is structured around a model of the T&D process. If your center has the luxury of this scenario, you are in luck— but both technical experts and management development expertise, as described in scenarios 1 and 2, will be needed. This allows the regional T&D function to deal with local units as whole organizations. So if you are performing a needs assessment, for example, and discover a deficiency in technical operations, you can assist in solving the problem in terms of both technical efficiency and managerial effectiveness. This enables the region to open discussions about providing programs that might seem less critical to the business from a technical point of view but that might be critical from an interpersonal perspective. Remember that criticality is determined by the perspective from which a deficiency is viewed. For example, things could be very critical from the corporate view but less urgent from the view of the local business unit. That can occur because local business units focus on execution and results, whereas corporate often takes a long-term and strategic view.

The holistic approach is preferable because it provides the greatest number of opportunities and growth for T&D professionals. All the elements in the model can be taken into account, allowing for more thorough and complete solutions. In this case, the region needs to have staff members who can see the values of both technical operations and management skills. There might also be opportunities to send people who have only technical skills with individuals with strong interpersonal skills to work on projects together, to learn from each other and pick up skills that they would learn more slowly by themselves.

One objective for the region is to have staff members teach their skills to one another. Staff members working on design projects might have the opportunity to work on both technical and management development programs. Using this holistic approach, the region should acquire a much broader perspective, develop technical skills, and minimize the perception that the region does not understand full business operations.

MATCH T&D STAFF TO TASKS

The preceding three scenarios indicate that staff should be matched to tasks. Two options seem appropriate in selecting staff. In one instance, new employees might be hired from outside the organization. The other option provides for the development of internal staff using carefully prepared materials.

Selecting Candidates

Prospective candidates who do not currently work for the company can be identified through the traditional methods of advertising in newspapers and magazines or through headhunters and other search firms. You might also post job openings on the Internet. Hire staff from the outside when the organization has an obvious skill gap. When the region deals with multiple client bases, hiring outside is usually the preferred choice. However, when you hire from the outside, greater effort must be put into defining the exact task requirements and the nature of relationships involved in the work. Discovering how well candidates demonstrate technical skills can be achieved by asking questions related to the ADDIE model to elicit experiences in analysis, design, development, implementation, and evaluation of training and development. Look for those who have experience in technical training in multiple locations and across different business units. The closer the experience matches your structure, the better the fit.

However, of the two skill requirements, technical and interpersonal, interpersonal skills are usually more important. Assessing the quality of interpersonal skills is tougher than determining technical skills, but not impossible. The first step is to interview candidates and allow them to reveal their interpersonal skills. This can be done by challenging them with a problem to solve and by asking open-ended questions about how they get along with other employees. Listen carefully for descriptions that represent less than tactful reactions and for comments that show lack of sensitivity to the differences among people.

Your company should have a profile of interaction styles of successful employees, so that the first task is to gauge how well the candidates meet the profile. A formal checklist can be used on which reactions are recorded, or the interviewer can simply write down key responses. In some cases, the most technically qualified person might not have the strongest interpersonal skills. To resolve ambiguities, other personnel should interview candidates. The more information secured early in the process, the more likely the best fit will be identified—but there is no guarantee. Sometimes mistakes are made, so involve people in the selection process who have some experience in selecting employees. Table 5.1 illustrates how you should record information about candidates for positions. It can be used for selecting employees both from inside and outside the business unit.

Selecting candidates from inside the company requires posting job requirements on the company's intranet. Information about their interpersonal competence might be more readily available. However, when people move from one function to another, it is possible they will respond differently to different circumstances. In fact, some employees might simply want to change areas because they have difficulty getting along with colleagues. There are no guarantees they will do better in training and development just because they are with the company now.

If the company handles a single product, it can mean that a transfer can be arranged more smoothly because the technical skills might be similar. However, if the company has multiple products, different skills might be required and the culture of units can be different; thus, the process might be very similar to selecting someone from outside the company. Hopefully, interactions with internal candidates give regional staff some ideas about

TABLE 5.1 Candidate Selection Chart

Name	Languages	Expertise Required	Internal/External	Expectations
Juan Salizar	Spanish, English	Marketing/sales background	Internal	No more than 2 years in the field before coming into corporate
Lisa Bonet	French, English, Italian	Operations experience at the managerial level	Internal	Has managed people in at least two areas
Woo Chang	Mandarin, English, French	Leadership development facilitation skills	External/internal	Strong facilitator and has to deal with senior management

the suitability of internal applicants. The interviewing staff might also want to talk to key stakeholders and future clients to gauge their comfort level with the candidate. As with external candidates, technical skills can be assessed by asking questions derived from the training model and the task requirements during the interview and then talking to others about the level of technical skills possessed by candidates.

Developing the T&D Staff

If the ideal candidate cannot be located, you might want to select individuals with relevant interpersonal skills and prepare them for T&D positions by means of a standardized training program. The training program can also be used to standardize training skills at both the regional and business unit levels. Regional staff will need to prepare professional materials carefully and establish a process for implementing the internal train-the-trainer program. The steps for designing such a program follow.

1. **Define the model**. To make it easier in this case, we suggest using the model described in Chapter 2. This allows all training personnel in the various markets within the organization to understand exactly what they need to do to improve their performance in the organization.

2. **Prepare the tools**. The task here is to provide specific tools, templates, and checklists about how each step (business input and T&D department, programs, and output) should be carried out. This enables common terms and data collection methodologies to be used and understood. Put them in a manual that contains examples of the tools so that everyone can see the standards and expectations of the training organization.

3. **Provide best practice**. Identify best practices for each training process, collect descriptions of them as examples, and prepare a "tool book." Teach the tool book to everyone involved so they understand how to execute the tools appropriately. In any case, make sure that staff in regional offices are practicing what they preach by implementing training procedures consistent with the guidelines.

4. **Evaluate behavior in terms of the model**. Have a process to evaluate what individuals are doing or, in the region's case, what you asked them to do. However, our experience shows that employees who know their work is being reviewed put a different emphasis on the outputs and align themselves with guidelines, standard tools, and specified processes while the review is conducted, but they revert to more convenient and comfortable practices afterward.

5. **Reward performance**. To ensure the tools become part of the organization's processes, give recognition to celebrate people' efforts. This helps encourage further participation and acceptance. The cost of implementing reward systems will be insignificant in comparison to the number of new and better processes being implemented and used.

FINANCING AND BUDGETING A REGIONAL T&D SYSTEM

Managing a business, in contrast to managing people, focuses primarily on financial issues, including income, expenses, purchases, inventory, cash flow, insurance, return on investment, debt, and profits. In T&D organizations, many additional financial issues must be decided, such as the construction of training facilities, the purchase of training equipment, staff salaries and expenses, project spending, translation of training materials, and communicating to store and office personnel, as well as to the public.

Finance is broadly defined as the activity concerned with planning, raising, controlling, and administering funds used in a business. Two issues—liquidity, the ability to pay current bills; and solvency, the ability to maintain long-term financial soundness—tend to dominate discussions of finance in business. Problems of finance are intimately connected with purchasing, production, and marketing, since success or failure in those areas is reflected in the financial condition and earnings of the business.

One of the first questions asked by organizations planning to set up a regional training function is, Should the function build facilities with "bricks and mortar," or should it operate like a virtual campus, without its own buildings and facilities? The question has no right or wrong answer; however, answering it requires addressing several internal and external factors.

Different elements come into play when a regional function tries to decide on housing, whether in new facilities or in currently available space. Facilities and equipment are often the largest budgetary line item in a T&D budget. Things such as depreciation, for example, might have a large budgetary effect during the first few years of operation. The expectation is the regional training manager might have some significant opinions on this topic. Minimally, all the possible issues should be presented for senior management to consider. Senior management usually has many questions that require detailed answers before decisions can be made. Thus, the costs must be calculated and justifications for these capital expenditures made.

Sometimes alternative housing plans might be viewed positively by the organization. Before you build, consider the possibility of sharing a facility with another educational or training provider. Consider whether other learning institutions (e.g., community colleges) could share their facilities. This option can give a quick and less costly start. Exploring the viability of this means finding a partner with whom to establish a joint campus. However, sharing might not be the preferred option for all organizations, since some don't like the idea of sharing a facility with other companies, regardless of cost savings. For those who choose this option, it could make an interesting community project.

Internally Focused Questions

When considering this important decision to build or not to build a physical facility, you will need to answer several internally focused questions. The first question is, Whose idea was it, and what was their reason for having a training center built? The answer to this query, in many cases, determines whether the center will be built. If the decision to build is being pushed from top management, it will probably get pushed through; if it isn't, the center will probably not get funded. With top management support, the training function only has to highlight issues from its perspective that would significantly affect the project.

A second question concerns whether space has already been proposed or designated in an existing building. If the choice is to use part of an existing company building, have contingencies been identified for the eventuality of the business suddenly expanding? Will the training floor space become a target for "takeover"? For the question of utilization, consider how the local population base will access the facilities. Also, will the current schedule of training programs meet the needs of the majority of the population? Consider how this will impact the utilization of the training rooms. Will all business unit heads agree to the funding model? Some business units might not support the project, question it outright, and challenge its true value. Watch for this and have a plan to satisfy these challenges. Getting this information will aid you in deciding how to secure a green light for building facilities.

From these questions, you should notice the difference among making the decision to have a center, having everyone agree to it, and ensuring that it survives as an ongoing training facility in the longer term. Planning for the eventualities posed by the questions will help shape strategies around funding, choice of locality, and facility utilization. Remember this may change again if a situation arises where there are senior leadership changes or the business climate shifts significantly. Be sure to have alternative plans to respond to such eventualities.

Externally Focused Questions

The picture will become clearer as answers are formulated around the internally focused questions. Nevertheless, the organization will also need to insert some externally focused questions into the equation as it decides whether to build. Here are some questions about external issues to think about: What are corporate headquarters' overall plans for the market and region? What is the company's purpose in building this facility? How will this impact employees, the general public, and the local government? What external marketplace factors are prompting you to have a regional training center? Does your major competitor have one? Is there a plan to use this to upstage your competition in a given market? Are there definite regulatory or tax benefits to building a facility the company can leverage?

Align with Corporate Plans

The more the facility falls within corporate plans, the greater chance of approval. From a top management perspective, a facility taking care of a significant customer/supplier or government constituency makes the facility more important. If corporate plans call for building training centers in each region, the stronger the case for making your facility a test to establish a footprint reproducible for other locations in the future.

The next question concerns where initial funding comes from. Are funds available from corporate headquarters? If not, the facility will probably need funding from business heads. This is significant, especially if the way the organization proposes to fund the center involves allocating costs back to the business unit. If so, you need to know whether the business heads support the cause. You will want to discover whether the center is expected to generate income to cover its costs or whether costs will be charged back to business units. If you have answers for these questions, the probability of endless debates, meetings, and discussions will lessen.

Scale of Facility

Another factor that will need to be resolved is the scale of a facility. What are the location and space requirements of the facility? This should be obvious. Do you need a two-room training center or a five-story regional training complex? The size needs to be balanced against affordability and purpose. Generally speaking, the smaller the project, the easier the sell. Whatever the size, remember to plan capacity for growth. Create a contingency plan showing adjacent areas or external facilities into which you can expand. This will help management understand the impact of capacity over a longer time frame and draw out reactions that show how much support there is for the facility in the long run.

All things equal, putting up a training facility is always a grand thing to do. And if done right, the center will provide business and shareholder returns. In most cases, having a physical facility demonstrates the company's commitment to employees' development and to the larger business community, enhancing the company's image of being a good corporate citizen.

Consider opening the facility to stage a public relations event. This can provide an avenue for senior management to involve local government officials in the pomp and pageantry of an opening ceremony. When CEOs, ambassadors, and senior government representatives are involved in an event that attracts media, the news coverage and acknowledgments have both tangible and intangible effects on the general public and current and potential employees. Companies should take advantage of training facility dedications since it is an opportunity to get free press while building a local and international image of being an "employer of choice" or "people developer." In some cases, building a facility that will be used to share knowledge with a local community enhances future business opportunities in the country. There are additional day-to-day points you need to address after you decide to build. We categorize and explain them as before and after building.

Before Building Before building consider commitment versus costs: Even before putting ideas on paper, find out from finance or other relevant source what amount of money can be made available for the project. This information is seen in conjunction with the company's forecasted revenues for the current and following years. This is important because constructing a state-of-the-art facility is expensive, usually costing millions of dollars. Develop an accurate forecast of all costs, including how the project will be managed so that costs will not balloon. Good business results combined with a sound project plan will assist in a positive decision process. The better the project forecast and business sentiment, the greater the chance of moving construction ahead.

As mentioned earlier, if the idea comes from the top, the project is usually assured. In this case, initial funding is not usually a problem. The only variable is its scale. Even if funding is secured, determine sentiment for the idea from as many regional executives as possible. This might impact ongoing debates on allocated depreciation costs to be covered by them. While obtaining this information, also establish the level of support among these executives for sending their staff to training, especially if the center is not in their region. The next task is to calculate the local population base, which will utilize at least 60 percent of the facility's capacity. This is important because you do not want to build a facility that demands everyone travel to use it. A ready population base is very important!

After Building Another question concerns whether the facility's upkeep will be organizationally funded or self-funded: Who is going to pay for ongoing expenses and depreciation charges? This goes beyond funding construction costs. It is usually easier to obtain seed money to build than to maintain the facility afterward. The headache typically comes in obtaining and generating revenues to cover ongoing costs.

Consider how overhead is to be funded. Will there be an expectation of ongoing funds from corporate headquarters to cover running costs? Or do you expect to cover these by collecting revenue from training fees charged to participants? Another option is to have the different business units in each region contribute to the running costs. If this is the decision, consider how costs will be calculated. Will using the number of employees or size of business be a fair method to apportion costs? What mechanism and time frame will be used to charge back costs to business units?

The answers to these questions determine where the regional T&D function's time will be spent. The function tends to focus on activities or services that generate the revenues to fund its activities. For example, if a majority of the revenues are obtained by conducting classes, then that activity will consume the majority of resources. This might be at the expense of supporting business units. It's not that one cannot perform both tasks, but you need a plan to finance and support the center.

The question of whether the facility should function as a profit or cost center also falls within the range of financial decisions. If the center becomes a profit center, the issues of pricing services and developing alternative sources of revenue become important financial issues.

When the decision to make the center a profit or cost function arrives, several issues must be resolved. If operating as a profit center, you will need to consider how to build a profit margin into the programs charged to internal clients. In addition, you must consider whether there is need for a separate pricing strategy for an external customer base. Pricing is a basic factor in ensuring profitability. The following questions are designed to help you gather information for determining how to price regional training services if it is to operate as a cost center:

1. Which regional operating costs remain the same regardless of sales volume?

2. Which operating costs decrease (in percentage) as sales volume increases?

3. What is the break-even point for each service at varying price levels?

4. Why do high gross-profit margins occur?

5. How do prices for services affect achieving a particular sales volume?

6. What is the target number of clients for next year?

7. Are record-keeping systems in place that give the needed data on profits, losses, and prices?

8. Do you regularly review pricing to ensure it is helping achieve profit goals?

In the beginning, you need to estimate your sales and expenses carefully. For example, to obtain a 30 percent margin on a service, you need to mark it up 42.9 percent. You might need to take the view that the price of all services provided to clients must cover all the costs of that particular program. This means that the price must include labor, materials, overhead—including design and production costs—and a predetermined percentage for profit.

Another way to determine prices is to take the full-costs approach but use those instead to establish a floor below which average prices are not allowed to fall. The costs become a reference point from which you can assign flexible prices in response to client demand and competition while still protecting against errors in pricing. Your mark-up goal is the difference between the cost price of services and the sales price of services, so you are able to achieve the following results: (1) cover operating expenses, (2) cover transportation costs, (3) provide net profit for the region, (4) provide for unexpected markdowns, and (5) inspire repeat business.

It is important to survey other parts of the organization to determine whether anyone is providing free training to the same target audience. Training is sometimes provided as part of an ongoing business product arrangement. If this is so, how will you reconcile providing free training for the same group to which others charge for services? This might sound esoteric, but we've come across training departments that face internal competition from others with the capability to provide free training. Nothing is wrong with this approach inherently; however, if the training department needs that revenue, guidelines will have to be spelled out clearly from the onset. For example, a consideration involving charging external vendors is whether their contracts require them to pay for training from the company. Do vendors have a choice, or are they bound by a contract/license or franchise agreement?

BUDGETING

Budgeting deals with the future, primarily in terms of finance. A budget helps determine whether a projected profit goal is within reach. A budget uncovers problems, suggests choices, and helps determine what changes to make to have a workable financial plan for the next year. In its simplest form, a budget is a detailed plan of expected future receipts and expenditures. Once the period you have budgeted for is completed, you can compare actual results with projected goals. If some expenses are higher than expected, start looking for ways to cut expenses or increase income. Costs tend to occur in three categories: fixed, variable, and semifixed. Semifixed costs have characteristics of both fixed and variable, so we will describe only fixed and variable costs in this context.

Fixed costs are items that do not vary with volume or productive activity. They accrue with the passage of time. They remain constant in amount for a given time period regardless of activity. Since these accrue over time, they should relate to a specified time period and be expressed as a constant each month or year. And they remain constant regardless of service quantity, but the cost per service provided changes inversely with the volume of services provided. Assume a fixed cost of $1,000. If 1,000 services are provided, the fixed cost per service is $1; however, if only 500 services are provided, the fixed cost per service is $2.

Variable costs are items that increase or reduce in proportion to volume or activity. They accrue as a result of productive effort or work performed. Variable costs would not exist if services were not delivered. Therefore, if activity doubles, the variable cost doubles. Because variable costs fluctuate in this way, some adequate measure of the activity of the department must be used. This is called the *activity base*. However, variable costs are related to units produced, which make them fixed per each unit of service delivered. Thus, assume variable costs of $1,000. If 1,000 services are provided, the variable cost per unit is $1. However, if 500 units of service are provided, the total variable cost is reduced to $500, with the variable cost per unit still remaining $1.

The effect of fixed and variable costs on a unit cost might be of considerable significance in many analyses of profits and losses and greatly affect management decisions concerning what services to deliver. In managing a regional training function, several items need to be budgeted— including travel expenses, project designs, program delivery, hardware and software, translation, overhead, and communication. Figure 5.3 presents an example of a departmental budget.

Some trade-offs might need to be made during the planning process, depending on what type of a budgeting process exists within the company. Are there fixed budgets, a zero-based budget, or partially funded budget options? The budget process that governs the regional center determines how much work is to be carried out at the center. We'll assume a scenario where you have a limited budget. A choice might need to be made between allocating funds

Department Budget				
	Q1	Q2	Q3	Q4
OVERHEADS				
Salaries				
Bonus				
Travel & Expenses				
Consultants				
Training & Education				
Communication/Media				
Others				
Subtotal				
DESIGN BUDGET				
Program A				
Program B				
Program C				
Subtotal				
DELIVERY				
Room				
Materials				
Instructors				
Travel				
Food & Beverage				
Gifts				
Other				
Subtotal				
TOTAL BUDGET				

FIGURE 5.3   Departmental Budget

to travel for business unit support or developing and marketing new programs.

Operational Overhead

Overhead refers to costs that are not included in direct material and labor, such as taxes, insurance, depreciation, power, supplies, utilities, and repairs. Operational overhead, as a rule, should be planned to consume no more than 50 percent of the budget. Wages, bonuses, and travel expenses should be captured as part of overhead, since they are a large part of the cost in meeting the needs of your constituents. This allows the other 50 percent to be used for the work of the department, which includes contracting work from external vendors, training delivery, and material translations. Communication costs should be budgeted separately.

There are several ways to work with external vendors. You can use them on a project-by-project basis or on contract. If you use vendors on a project basis, clear guidelines must be established early to manage this situation.

Such guidelines should include nondisclosure agreements (Fig. 5.4) and project management schedules for the beginning of the project. A set of design templates—including objective matrices, program outlines, and design documents—must be created in a particular format. This helps the organization not only manage the various vendors but also get used to a structured way of designing training programs. Design documents should be used to clarify your thinking about a specified course.

An easier method is to locate a design firm that could provide a range of personnel from instructional designers to production or graphic artists. Together you can negotiate a contract based on the region's total development needs. This way you only deal with one vendor and have

1. **Effective Date.** This agreement ("Agreement") shall be deemed effective as of _____. __, the first day of my association with xxxxxxxxxx (the Company) personally and on behalf of xxxxxx.

2. **Confidentiality.** I will maintain in confidence and will not disclose or use, either during or after the term of my association with xxxxxxxxxx or any of its affiliates, any proprietary or confidential information or know-how belonging to the Company for five (5) years from the date of acquisition whether or not in written form, except to the extent required to perform duties on behalf of the Company. Proprietary Information refers to any information, not generally known in the relevant trade or industry, which was obtained from the Company, or which was learned, discovered, developed, conceived, originated, or prepared by me in the scope of my association on behalf of xxxxxxxxxx and shall include, but not be limited to research, development, or marketing plans, financial, cost, price, technical, or test data; formulations, inventions, designs, products, or processes. Proprietary Information shall not include any information that is expressly approved for release by xxxxx, disclosed in a product marketed by xxxxx already publicly or legitimately known or legitimately, independently developed by me prior to xxxxx disclosure, or information that is furnished to others without similar restrictions. Upon completion of my assignment(s) I will deliver to the Company all written and tangible material in my possession incorporating any Proprietary Information or otherwise relating to the Company's business. I will not retain any copies of any documents or materials furnished to me by the Company or prepared by me for the Company.

3. **Nonsolicitation.** During the term of my association with the company for a period of one (1) year thereafter, I will not solicit or encourage, or cause others to solicit or encourage, any employees of the Company to terminate their employment with the Company. During that same period, I will not solicit or encourage, or cause others to solicit or encourage, the business of any current or then-current customer of the Company.

4. **Termination.** I acknowledge and agree that my association with the Company is for no specified term and may be terminated by me or the Company at any time, with or without cause.

Agreed this _____ day of _____, _____.

_____

(Contractor's Signature)

Agreed this _____ day of _____, _____.

_____

(xxxxxx Representative)

FIGURE 5.4 Nondisclosure Document

more leverage. Over time, as the vendor becomes familiar with the company's business, it will become more effective at delivering a high-quality product that matches the organization's needs with shorter cycle times.

External vendors may also be a good bridge in developing skills of the training team. For example, external vendors might provide multiple language capabilities for translation and delivery of training. When done right, your vendors should fit seamlessly into the training organization and become indistinguishable from company personnel.

Materials Translation

When operating in a region with many ethnic or cultural backgrounds, materials translation becomes a significant issue. Many times, companies wonder whether they should be translating. But if translation is a requirement for running your business, you must do it. If you don't, you might find yourself preparing materials in one language with the hope that the markets will do their own translating. Allowing translation to occur in this way has the inherent risk of uncontrolled variability. There is nothing inherently wrong with giving control over translations to individual markets, but such an approach gives them the ability to practice the "not invented here syndrome" and inadvertently change the original intent of training materials.

One way of controlling the quality of translations is to control its budget. Simply set criteria for receiving pay for translation projects and require that the process be followed before funds are released. This is a good way of ensuring compliance. The markets feel they are getting a better product because they exercise control over translations, and the image of the regional training organization is enhanced.

Communication

Communication is probably the most important aspect and, sometimes, the least paid attention to as a separate budget item. Communication is maintained as a separate budget line to ensure that it gets the appropriate attention. If you have a great product and no one knows about it, it is of little value. Moreover, if you do good and no one knows about it, you might as well have not done it; develop a plan of attack to heighten awareness within the organization of all the activity in the T&D function. In many cases, it is not the actual medium that is important but the clarity and regularity of the message. Chapter 3 contains a section devoted to communication strategies and vehicles for organizational communication.

COST MODELS

In a company, a philosophical point of view about "who pays for what" must exist. A critical question that grows out of this involves whether the organization treats training as an investment or simply a cost for the company. The company might be prepared to cover fixed overhead costs like design and development and charge only for the variable training costs such as delivery to participants. This is a good compromise in a start-up.

On the other hand, prevalent thought in the organization might be that the company needs to be lean and return a high percentage to its shareholders. This might mean it wants to recover all costs for training activities, including fixed overhead. In such cases, you should consider charging back an allocated percentage of the running costs to the various markets rather than trying to generate revenue for each program.

Once you decide whether the training function is to be a cost or profit center, the rest is quite straightforward. Construct a cost model for the following: (1) facilities, (2) staff, (3) development, (4) translation, and (5) fixed costs or overhead. Then determine how to recover costs by pricing programs accordingly. Also consider how this charging mechanism will work. Will training fees be charged back to designated accounts, or will you be able to collect using credit cards? We recommend you keep an accurate tab on a monthly basis to ensure accurate accounting of funds.

PRICING T&D SERVICES

There is no formula except that whichever model you choose you need to ensure that the pricing model covers the budget.

Option A: Fully funded. This means you build a budget and submit it on a yearly basis and work in those constraints. Under this option, training could be theoretically free, or at no cost, to participants. However, this practice could be abused, as no pain (loss of money) does not result for not showing up. This often means that the value of the information is not seen as good to outside vendors. This is more psychological than real, but it is probably based on historical company practices. There are other ways of minimizing no-shows, including publishing names, departments, or business units in training reports. If you want to keep the model neat for option A, provide training at no cost.

Option B: Partially funded. In this option, the organization funds the overhead and design and development, but the delivery of training is based on cost recovery. This means you must determine the cost of a training program, regardless of length. Then you take the total program cost and divide it by the length (e.g., number of days) of the program. The result is an accurate per-day cost for offering the event. This way all costs associated with the different programs can be determined and a price set for each program. It might be necessary to use the methods of calculation illustrated in Figure 5.5 for each market in which the training program is offered. This method creates a differentiated price structure for each market. A way to simplify the price variability is to use a single, per-day charge. Prospects will then know that if it is a two-day program, they will be charged two times the basic charge, and a five-day program is five times the base charge. This method is easily understood and implemented.

Option C: Not funded. This means that you must recover all costs for the entire training budget. This is achieved by adding a fixed percentage to the full cost of the program. This model presumes that you are running a mini–commercial training organization within the company.

As in any small company, you should keep costs down and services priced so that total revenues cover total expenses. This is interesting because internal clients discover that services must be priced according to comparable programs in the open market. The alternative is to take the market price as a benchmark and give a discount. This is done because your internal customers expect that they should receive a price break from an internal department. If the department is not able to cover its costs, this can mean one of two things: Costs are too high, or prices are too low. If you are above or at market price and cannot cover costs, reevaluate what the T&D function is doing. This is a sign that something is wrong.

Fixed Costs

Instructor fee		3000
Airfare		400
Advertising		
Room charges		
AV equipment		100
	Subtotal A	3500

Variable Costs

Participant guides		65
Food and beverage		100
Giveaways		
Other		
	Subtotal B	165
Proposed Fee	C	500
Number of participants/ Revenue (15*C)		7500
Total Cost (A+B*15)		5975
Profit		1525
Contribution (C–B)	D	335
Number of participants/ to Breakeven (A/D)		10.44

FIGURE 5.5 Pricing Model

SOURCES OF REVENUE

There are only so many things the T&D function can do to establish sources of revenue; we list here a few sources with commentary. Every company has limitations and boundaries on what the training function can do, so you need to have several options available.

1. **Charge for programs**. This is the most obvious way to recover costs and generate revenue. Whether or not the regional training center has a monopoly on providing services should be considered. What you can charge for services might depend on your customers and what they will allow you to charge. Finding the right price is tougher than it might seem.

2. **Charge for consulting services**. In addition to providing programs, training departments might also offer consulting services on how to facilitate meetings, performing process mapping, team building, mentoring, and other services for which it could bill. The key to this source being available is the caliber of your personnel.

3. **Charge for materials**. Create a list of published materials that could be purchased through a catalog of materials. These materials could be participant or instructor guides that support existing programs. Job aids or company published materials could also be included.

4. **Charge for development work**. Charge for the development work the T&D function would do for various departments that require professionally developed materials.

5. **Develop external services**. One way to develop revenue is to make programs available to suppliers and customers of the organization. This still might be politically correct with business leaders. Making programs available to the general public is the next step, which is only as good as your training and materials.

6. **Obtain government funding**. Many countries have funds available for companies that train employees

in the form of matching or other grants. They have usually criteria for obtaining these funds, so efforts to understand the criteria can result in obtaining these funds.

7. **Seek sponsorship from vendors and suppliers**. Many vendors and suppliers can sponsor breaks, lunches, or dinners at training events. Another option is for vendors to provide training materials that include their products. Even though this might not be direct revenue, the savings can help lower overall expenses while still maintaining the revenue collected.

Cautions about Raising Revenue

The first caution is to rethink whether external training can be justified as part of the regional training center's mission. Does the mission describe the target audience the center is to serve? Does the mission clearly indicate the center is to provide support only to the markets and business units in the region, or does it include providing services to external partners? Even if the mission does include external partners, the current regional team might not have the capability to provide high-level services to external partners. If you have experienced training personnel to provide services, you might discover that the demand for those types of services increases. In fact, your staff might enjoy working with external clients more than internal ones as external clients view them as experts and sometimes give them more respect. Finally, by raising revenue from the outside, the function becomes accustomed to the revenue, and it might become difficult to turn your back on it. Trainers might enjoy it because they see new challenges each time and get to meet different people.

INTERNET CONSIDERATIONS

Several learning and knowledge management systems software programs have extensive reporting capability ranging from cost models to profit and loss statements. A few of these packages were mentioned in Chapter 4. Because each organization tends to emphasize different aspects of its budget, you should choose a program that is most appropriate for your needs. Most of these programs can be accessed through the Internet by the "Web connect" feature included in the packages.

Using these packages to manage training administration is usually more economical than a manual or nonintegrated computer system, since fewer people are needed to manage the details. These full-service programs allow you to track both traditional and Web-based training for your employees, as well as external partners who might need accurate records to track certification requirements. The Internet allows you to reach employees and also partners, vendors, and franchisees, which might enable you to spread the costs for generic Web-based program over a larger number of trainees.

CONCLUSION

We have seen then that the regional training function has unique characteristics. Relationships with corporate will vary based on the amount of control versus autonomy assigned to the region. Regions follow corporate mandates and standards but exercise more control over regional and local unit functions, especially at the operations level. Relationships with other regions may best be described as strategic alliances where each regional office is part of a loosely coupled system in which they support each other in a collegial way. The internal structure of a regional function is no less unique. While size and internal structure drive staffing, the key to success lies in following a model for selecting and preparing the staff. The larger decision regarding whether to build a freestanding regional facility brings together both internal and external considerations involving funding of the center, pricing, and revenue streams. Whether housed in a freestanding facility or operating as a virtual center with limited staff, the regional center becomes a center of information and activity uniting the various arms of the multiple-location system.

HOW TO ASSESS PERFORMANCE

*Measuring the return on investment (ROI)
in training and development has consistently
earned a place among the critical issues in the
Human Resource Development (HRD) field. . . .
Although the interest in the topic has heightened
and much progress has been made, it is still an
issue that challenges even the most sophisticated and progressive HRD departments.*

JACK J. PHILLIPS

Conducting a regular audit is one of the most powerful ways to sustain a multiple-location training system. In this chapter we will describe exactly how to assess and review a multiple-location system and use assessment tools throughout the centers. Once you are comfortable with the tools, you can begin using the assessment results to develop local units using a teaching/consulting approach. Do you want to know whether the multiple-location system is being followed and how it is working? Then you must measure.

Whether the process is called a *review,* a *measure,* or an *evaluation,* each term means the same thing in this context, and each represents a systematic way of looking at the accomplishments of the various training organizations and their people. We recommend the system review document (Figure 6.1). Using this document at headquarters before you

	Scoring		
3 = We continually do this and do it well. 2 = We are actively focused on developing in this area. 1 = We could use some help here.	**3**	**2**	**1**
Analysis/Business Input Phase **Environmental Scan** 1. Have you benchmarked your training initiatives against the performance of other business units?			
2. Have you benchmarked your training initiatives against your competitors?			
3. Have you evaluated all PESTLE elements, internal and external (political, economic, social, technological, legal, and environmental)?			
Business Objectives 1. Have you reviewed the business objectives of your business unit?			
2. Have you identified those that you can favorably impact this year?			
3. Have you aligned the objectives of the T&D organization with those of the business unit and other organizations?			
HR Requirements 1. Have you developed or do you regularly review manpower-planning data as a means of forecasting future training load?			
2. Have you developed or do you regularly review performance appraisal or competency data as a means of forecasting future training load?			
3. Have you encouraged/supported line supervisors and managers in carrying out their responsibility for training?			
	(Continued)		

FIGURE 6.1 System Review Document

3 = We continually do this and do it well.
2 = We are actively focused on developing in this area.
1 = We could use some help here.

	Scoring		
	3	2	1
Target Group Profiles 1. Have you created a profile of your target group segmented by job titles, competencies, and headcount?			
2. Are these profiles used at the analysis phase of ADDIE?			
Skills/Competencies 1. Have you identified ways of measuring competence gaps?			
2. How do you ensure that the appropriate personnel attend programs?			
Design/Organizational Structure Phase **Vision and Values** 1. Have you published or otherwise circulated your defined vision, goals, and objectives statements?			
2. Were key stakeholders external to the department involved in the development of the vision, goals, and objectives statements for the training department?			
3. How widely have these statements been communicated within the organization?			
Goals and Objectives 1. Are the vision, goals, and objectives aligned with the organizational business objectives?			
2. Have you asked key stakeholders to identify critical issues that could be favorably impacted by training initiatives?			

FIGURE 6.1 Continued

	Scoring		
	3	2	1
3. How do you review your training department's goals in light of changing business requirements?			
Infrastructure and Process 1. Do you conduct a periodic review of your organizational structure to ensure that goals are met?			
2. Do you have financial systems in place to ensure that resources and funding are sufficient and properly monitored?			
3. Do you have adequate facilities and facilities management to offer a positive learning environment?			
4. Do you have a communication process in place that raises the visibility of training initiatives (newsletters, bulletins, catalogs, brochures)?			
5. Do you have a policies and procedures handbook which clearly outlines philosophy, policies, practices, and standards?			
6. Do you have a process in place for ensuring that T&D practitioners have the skills and knowledge needed to fulfill their roles?			
Training System Review and Rewards 1. Do you engage in an annual review of the training organization and all its components?			
2. Do you utilize a standard review format and forms for these annual evaluations?			
3. Do you have a formal award system in place for those inside and outside the organization who contributed to training excellence?			
	(Continued)		

	Scoring		
3 = We continually do this and do it well. 2 = We are actively focused on developing in this area. 1 = We could use some help here.			
	3	2	1
Development/Products and Services Phase **Curriculum/Program Planning**			
1. How do you ensure that you are providing high-priority, high-payoff interventions?			
2. Do you provide ancillary services such as coaching and mentoring?			
3. Do you intentionally and routinely ask yourselves whether training is the most effective intervention in each situation?			
4. Do you use the ADDIE process to guide the creation of each new course or intervention?			
5. Do you intentionally and regularly incorporate new training techniques into courses?			
6. How do you ensure that T&D interventions are not duplicated in other places in the organization?			
Program Logistics and Administration 1. Do you use learning or training management systems to gain efficiencies and accomplish record keeping of participant and course records?			
2. Do you have a registration system that is easy to use?			
3. Do you track participant reaction to course administration and logistic procedures?			
Program Materials 1. Are learning objectives and evaluation measures linked to all courses?			

FIGURE 6.1   Continued

	Scoring		
	3	2	1
2. Are courses/programs documented with a fully developed instructor's guide and participants' manual when appropriate?			
3. Do you use a design template or style guide to standardize the look and feel of training materials and provide maximum efficiency in development?			
Delivery Mechanisms and Equipment 1. What new technologies/delivery mechanisms have you adopted this year?			
2. How is T&D staying abreast of new technologies (VR, Internet, CD, interactives)?			
3. Do instructors have the equipment they need to deliver the quality of programs they are capable of delivering?			
4. How do you provide all necessary logistics and feedback for employees who want to complete Web-based or other self-paced learning?			
Implementation/Execution Phase **Learning Environment** 1. Do you ensure that classrooms provide appropriate quality of space, noise control, ventilation, and comfort?			
2. Do you have a vehicle for encouraging employees and staff to generate new ideas, take risks, and experiment?			
3. Are staff/learners recognized and rewarded for completing learning interventions?			
Instructors and Staff 1. Do you have sufficient instructors with the competencies needed to deliver the programs offered?			
			(Continued)

	Scoring		
3 = We continually do this and do it well. 2 = We are actively focused on developing in this area. 1 = We could use some help here.	3	2	1
Instructors and Staff 2. Are trainers' evaluations consistently used and the results communicated?			
3. How do you ensure that staff and instructors are well managed and understand performance standards?			
4. Are reporting relationships clearly understood and defined?			
5. What efforts do you make to ensure good relationships and trust among your training team members?			
6. If external vendors are used, how do you ensure transfer of learning into the organization?			
Learning Process 1. Do you carefully consider the audience to whom you are bringing the subject?			
2. How do you ensure that employees and their managers prepare for and follow up on learning opportunities?			
3. How are the staff keeping touch with the latest training trends, technologies/methods (e.g., WBT, NLP)?			
4. Do you experiment by introducing new training techniques in programs?			
Evaluation/System Output Phase **Impact on Business Performance** 1. Is the feedback form used at the end of each course/intervention (level 1)?			

FIGURE 6.1   Continued

	Scoring		
	3	2	1
2. Do you assess mastery of learning objectives at the end of each course/intervention? (Level 2)			
3. Do you assess the application of what was learned to on-the-job performance? (Level 3)			
4. Do you assess the impact of training on the business? (Level 4)			
5. Do you communicate the impact of T&D to key stakeholders?			

examine what the locations are doing is important because it shows your colleagues that gap analysis is not just for the "little" guys. The story of the old shoemaker applies well here. You may recall that the old shoemaker made shoes for everyone in the village. But his own children had no shoes. In just the same way the training director reviews his own processes and products before he says anything about other people's operations.

You might be tempted to administer a questionnaire to determine how well the various training and development functions have been doing. But we urge you to put the model in place and then assess local training organizations according to the fifteen elements grouped within the following five areas described in Chapter 2: analysis/ business input, design/organizational structure, development/ products and services, implementation/execution, and evaluation/system/output. It is best to practice what you preach, so go through the process of building the system before you try to assess it or get others to use it.

Being pragmatic, though, you understand your situation and the implementation strategies that may work best in the company's operations in different geographic locations. Hence, we want to describe how we think the review and assessment process should work, and you can compare your ideas.

WHY ADMINISTER THE REVIEW DOCUMENT?

After building your system from the beginning, following the steps in Chapter 2, you are now ready to see how the system is performing. If anything is out of alignment, you can adjust the T&D system so that it is consistent with your plans. We'll assume that the system is in place. The first evaluation is to establish the yearly review process. Why? Let's look at a common dilemma faced by many headquarters staff.

You get into a market. You give some advice. You stipulate some procedures and get agreement. You conduct some training. However, after you leave, in many cases, little or nothing is done. You move on to the next market and repeat the process.

This may seem extreme, especially where training managers in the markets have only a dotted-line reporting relationship to the headquarters T&D function. If your organization (region/division) is situated closer to the multiple locations (markets), your efforts may be more effective. Nevertheless, we know that working people are busy doing what their immediate bosses instruct. If you visit frequently or are on the phone enough, you can apply pressure to move individuals in a local market to implement some of the suggested ideas. However, the more markets you have, the fewer trips and phone calls you can make. Reality suggests that a third-quarter travel freeze—due to cost control measures—could obstruct your best-intentioned travel plans.

For this example, we'll assume that the market you just visited remains status quo. Do you know the old adage "What you measure is what gets done"? Most training professionals teach this concept but often fail to use it in their own work. Since we are functioning on the basis of a broader systems concept, we could say that the actions you *define, train, assess, and reward* are what get done on a consistent basis throughout the organization.

The evaluation strategy we describe next is really very simple, and it is based on the DTAR (define, train, assess, and reward) philosophy. The first task, therefore, is to define the system, which we did in Chapter 2. The second task is to ensure that you have the training available. Being prepared with a full complement of training and development approaches takes away the excuses that employees don't know what to do, how to do it, or when to do it. Corporate training and development provides multiple-location training units with the tools and templates to do their work. The third task is to establish a review mechanism and process. This provides an evaluation and a basis for rewarding those who meet the standards.

Why does this process work? When you announce that awards will be presented for outstanding performance, employees often respond with excitement, especially when they feel they are competing for authentic honors. Other employees respond to avoid embarrassment, especially if they feel they are less prepared now; however, if they have an opportunity to improve before the evaluation occurs, embarrassment may be significantly reduced. This is especially true when the evaluation team is well respected and knows what it is doing. Tricon Restaurants International has implemented a training and development review process that confirms this assumption about the effect of measurement on performance.

What is the best way to introduce a review process? In most cases, it is presented most effectively during a regional, divisional, or worldwide T&D conference. To achieve the strongest impact, distribute information in advance explaining that you have defined a T&D system and are providing some guidelines and tools that will aid the markets to enhance their performance and overall capability. Then announce, after the markets have had an opportunity to study the guidelines and use the tools, that a "training and development review team" will conduct an audit to see how well they are doing. Mention that individuals and local teams that do the very best in implementing the guidelines and practices will receive "The Training and Development Award."

The review process has other benefits; during the review is a good time to share best practices and suggest ways a team in one market can adopt practices from another. An occasional problem arises when you introduce the idea of best practices. Some markets are sensitive to the "not invented here" syndrome. If they didn't think of it, they won't use it. Many times, you can avoid the syndrome by mentioning that you "know of some companies that . . ." and describe a best practice; or you might say, "Over the years, our experience has shown that . . ." and introduce the best practice from some other market.

HOW TO ADMINISTER THE REVIEW DOCUMENT

The audit questionnaire, called the *T&D review document*, consists of a set of questions that match each of the fifteen elements in Figure 2.1. Although the responses are unique to each company in each market, the questionnaire has been standardized for ease of administration and interpretation of data. The review team should be able to answer these questions satisfactorily before expecting others to answer them.

In fact, if you want uniformity among all of the locations in the system, you are more likely to achieve it if a regional office or headquarters uses the same processes and tools that market T&D functions in the field are expected to use. Carefully study the T&D review document presented in Figure 6.1 to see what it entails.

The review process is designed to enable all locations in the system to understand what is required and the standards they should maintain. The process should also establish clear performance standards for the T&D function. It also allows the review team from headquarters to assess the current performance of regional and divisional functions against these standards so as to identify gaps in the T&D function at all levels in the organization.

The action plan that results from the process shows that the training and development teams are working on the right priorities to support organizational goals. It also provides a way to monitor and track the various markets under your review and to know which ones need more attention.

Introduce the review process by explaining the questionnaire during a suitable forum such as a training and development meeting at which all leaders of T&D functions are present. Establish early the requirement that participants are to go through the questionnaire with their teams before the next visit by the review team. Also indicate when the review dates are scheduled, which should be at least four to six months in advance of the rollout, to give them time to prepare for your arrival.

Send the questionnaire to the training teams ahead of time, or place it on your Web site as described at the end of the chapter, so that they can do a self-assessment and score the document. Ask them to gather evidence to support their claims. For example, if local trainers indicate that they have a vision statement, they must be able to show you the written statement during the review and identify others, and not simply themselves, who know about the vision statement. The review team has the responsibility to assess how widely the particular knowledge, skill, or process, and particular pieces of information, are distributed among those in the T&D function. For example, how widely has the local training and development vision been communicated?

During the review process, the review team members should go through the questionnaire item by item asking for the scores the local team gave themselves. Evidence to support their claims needs to be provided. Together, the review team and the local T&D team should come to an agreement on the score that they are to receive. The final score should be based on the experience of the review team with other markets and how the market being reviewed compares with others according to review document standards. The process may take two to three hours, with more time spent on the initial questions and less time on later ones, with the rate of coverage speeding up toward the middle of the questionnaire. This is usually the case since several questions share similar root answers.

FOLLOW-UP ACTION PLANS

After the scores have been determined, the review and local teams identify performance gaps and devise a plan to assist the local team to improve performance. Immediately following this meeting, a short report indicating the results of the review should be prepared and delivered to the manager of the T&D function. This report should document the process and indicate how the review team will assist the market. Report preparation usually takes half a day, depending on how much discussion occurs around current processes, procedures, and action plans.

After the review team has completed three or four market reviews, make a comparative analysis by posting the scores given to each market and calibrating the scoring procedures. When you're satisfied that the review process is consistent, then complete the training review for all participating locations. The term *participating* is used here because, with the initial reviews, some markets may feel they are so far off the mark that they may simply decline to participate. Nevertheless, you still need to decide whether to review those markets, because it may help the training team focus on its best opportunities. You are now ready to select the market with the best score and recognize it with the "Training and Development Award." Corporate may also want to establish score ranges for gold, silver, and bronze categories, and give awards to all units that qualify within those ranges.

Whatever approach is used, remember that when awards are presented, pride of the local units is at stake. People put effort into preparing for these reviews, especially if they recognize that the process is very important to the organization. It is also good to let local senior managers know about and participate in the awards program. If upper management has a stake in the outcome, they will support the efforts of the local T&D team in preparing for the review. In some cases, this is where local T&D managers might ask for additional resources to increase their chances for having a good review.

When possible, awards should be presented at a forum in which both the T&D community and senior management are present. After that, communicate who won and why to the rest of the organization. This approach gives the participants added recognition and visibility. The ultimate outcome is to get training and development in the markets aligned more precisely. As a final reminder, the seven steps in the review process may be summarized as follows:

1. Introduce the process.
2. Prepare the market team for the review meeting.
3. The review team meets with the market team.
4. Both teams come to agreement on the final score.
5. The review team identifies the assistance they can provide.
6. The review team recognizes the top achievers in all markets.
7. The results are communicated throughout the organization.

How do you communicate the results to the organization? One suggestion is to highlight the yearly training and development conference in an upcoming company newsletter. Announce that at the end of the year, an award for the best T&D team, based on guidelines for having a quality training and development function, will be awarded.

Talk about the questions to be used as the basis for the review. By then, training managers should have received the questions. Point out that the questionnaire follows the T&D system that was introduced to each market unit. Using this sequence, the review process seems more logical.

You may also want to explain that a handbook of tools and procedures is being published for use in preparing answers for the review questions. The newsletter reports are as much, if not more, for the people who are not in the T&D function. A newsletter feature can provide an overview of what you are trying to achieve in the organization and familiarize people with a consistent approach to running the total T&D function. When the training and development teams use the review, you will be able to collect data to show that the model described in

Chapter 2 does work to drive consistency and standardization throughout the organization.

TEACH AND CONSULT TO SUPPORT THE SYSTEM

With the audit process in place, you—the T&D function leader—now have a structured way to assess gaps. You also have an avenue to provide coaching for the training and development managers in the various distribution lines throughout the organization. To move ahead, you can do several things. For markets that haven't completed the review, you can visit them and help them prepare for a review. For those who have completed the review, you help them work on narrowing the biggest gaps. During the review, you can give advice to local managers concerning how they can best develop their own skills to affect change in their units.

You should keep a file on each market with notes about strengths and weaknesses. This gives you a list of things to talk about as you follow up with each market. Having notes available makes it easier for you to provide specific assistance. In addition, managers feel comfortable with you and value your advice.

You should also keep a file of best practices for each box in the system model (see Chap. 2), which you should put into a database. This helps compile a list of ideas and workable solutions to problems that may surface when specific support requests are made from a market.

If you have not been able to identify key gaps, the business plans for individual markets should be a source of ideas for a yearly plan of action. Repeating the review process on a six-month or yearly basis (depending on your resources) allows you to align all the multiple locations so that everyone has common tools and practices. This helps you become aware of the "health" of the T&D teams in the organization. Continued use of the review should create a continuous improvement process for the T&D function. Keep highlighting the yearly recipient of the training award through newsletters and senior management involvement. Like any profession or skill, the more you do it, the better you get.

For many, the faster you start doing the right things, the quicker you bring them about. Where this review document has been used, T&D managers are thankful for a guide to focus their activities. Even if they are not doing everything they want right now, they know what is missing. They can avoid doing the same thing over and over with limited results. For locations that are operating at a more advanced level, feel free to add more questions or even new categories to the list. Remember that it's the strategy of define, teach, assess, and reward that you are attempting to implement, not the appropriateness of any particular or specific question.

DEPLOYING THE SYSTEM REVIEW ON THE INTERNET

The training audit, or any of the functional audits discussed earlier, is relatively simple to deploy on the Internet. Consider the following scenario: You are a market-level training manager who has received word from the training director of her immediate visit to your location. You log on to the company training Web site and click on functional reviews. Once there, you choose the training review, paying particular attention to any questions added since the last review. After you have completed the review, the program automatically generates a baseline document that highlights areas of strength and weakness.

You press the Submit button, and the baseline report is automatically submitted to the training director to whom you report. The director receives your scores and prepares her thoughts for the planned meeting or begins an e-mail correspondence to support you. She also prepares additional information to support you in strengthening areas of weakness. Her resources may include journal articles, best practices from other training organizations, or the names of colleagues who could be helpful. Meanwhile, you print a copy and discuss the results with your team. The review shows an icon in the column next to each question. The team revisits the tools and resources linked to that icon and makes the necessary adjustments in procedure while awaiting the on-site visit.

In this scenario the company still uses good old-fashioned face-to-face meetings for the actual review. But completing the system review prior to the meeting has saved a lot of time. If you'd like, the actual review can be done through a synchronous Internet meeting by means of computers or video conferencing. Even if technology allows you to complete a distant review, you still need the face-to-face meeting to establish and maintain relationships and build culture.

CONCLUSION

The system review document sits at the heart of establishing and maintaining a high-performance T&D function. What is its purpose? To measure performance against a baseline, assess compliance with the system, and motivate employees, and reward accomplishment. In a multiple-locations system, there is simply no other way to accomplish all this in a cost- and time-effective way. Growth and development can only occur when managers and employees know what is expected, have the tools necessary to meet those expectations, and are motivated by the promise of rewards. The beauty of the process and tool described involves primary stakeholders and uses their natural talents, allowing them the opportunity to develop without overt criticism Few evaluation systems achieve their goals in a fashion that enhances the self-respect and confidence of employees. This audit process makes a review supportive of self-respect and enhances the confidence of employees.

CHAPTER 7

HOW TO ENSURE SURVIVAL

*It must be remembered that there is nothing
more difficult to plan, more doubtful of success,
nor more dangerous to manage, than the creation of a new system. For the initiator has the
enmity of all who would profit by the preserva-
tion of the old institutions and merely luke-
warm defenders in those who would gain by
the new ones.*

MACHIAVELLI

With the multiple-location system and system
review document developed and operational, the next step
is to implement survival plans to ensure that all locations
know how to operate skillfully within their political environment. As you know, the best training and development
plans amount to little unless each field location is able to
build bridges to critical power centers at all levels of the
organization. In this chapter, we will look at nine critical
success factors covering the gamut from planning to attitude
to reliability. We will look at the creative tension between
performance and politics and offer a case study on how
that dynamic can derail your success. Finally, we will
investigate how to respond to too many requests made too
often and on too short a notice. Sound familiar?

A RELATIONSHIP GRID

Those leaders who survive in an organization over a period of time use relationship-building skills to build influence. A good way to determine whether the field locations are doing enough in the relationship-management dimension is to check their actions against a relationship grid. A relationship grid allows you to determine whether training and development employees are building effective organizational relationships. This is achieved by analyzing their actions according to three key dimensions with three critical success factors each—for a total of nine (Fig. 7.1). The first dimension is *involvement*, with planning, communication, and recognition as its success factors. The second dimension is *capability*, which includes individual, functional, and organizational success factors. *Respect* is the third dimension and involves integrity, reliability, and results.

INVOLVEMENT: PLANNING, COMMUNICATION, RECOGNITION

Planning

Involvement can be increased in the early stages of establishing the T&D system by ensuring that every key leader at each location has input in the planning process. This should begin with data gathering as part of the environmental scan and the statement of business objectives (see Chap. 2). This may be done by gathering input from everyone through one-on-one sessions as part of the needs assessment stage. Have extended off-site meetings for personnel in operational functions that have the greatest potential for gains from T&D products and services. People also tend to participate more fully when meetings are organized with a clear agenda and expected outputs.

	Critical Success Factors		
Involvement:	Planning	Communication	Recognition
Capability:	Individual	Functional	Organizational
Respect:	Integrity	Reliability	Results

(Dimensions)

FIGURE 7.1   Relationship Grid

Involvement in this way allows managers and workers to feel they have an influence on the process of devising the basic business strategy.

Another way to involve employees in the planning process is to prepare some plans and then solicit feedback from workers and managers in the various business units about their viability. Focus groups can be used to review the plans to demonstrate full involvement. This way, you establish a pattern of involving people in the planning process, which allows you to obtain feedback from more organization members and even customers. And most will also be familiar with the plans that the T&D function is heading.

With this type of extensive involvement, you should be able to adjust the direction or convince colleagues that the planned direction is the right path. It is best to decide in advance whether the sessions are going to be purely feedback oriented or "persuasion sessions." If they are the latter, you will need to do a lot of groundwork with the participants before they come to the session. This consists of holding many meetings before the meeting. If you want authentic feedback, plan the meeting for just that purpose, and avoid giving reasons for why things have to go in any particular direction. Your posture should be one that shows you're really listening for inputs.

Communication

Plan to have a comprehensive communication strategy that covers all of your key constituents. This should include the use of several different methods to reach them. More important than the message, however, is ensuring that they receive information on a regular basis. Consistent and regular information garners a lot more credibility than starting something that fizzles. The methods by which organization members can be kept informed are myriad. For example, information may be distributed by reports and newsletters— via e-mail and hard copy—catalogs, calendars, surveys, video messages, phone messages, session announcements, and follow-ups to both participants and supervisors. The communication goal is to reach each person from your customer base using at least three different forms four times a year, minimally. Where organization members have extensive Internet accessibility and use, the frequency of messages can go up dramatically without much additional effort. The point is to have descriptions of the products and services of the T&D function visible.

By using both electronic and traditional methods of communicating information throughout the organization, the T&D function will go a long way toward gaining the reputation required for doing its job. Communicating the "story" of the T&D function is an important strategy that needs to be thought through carefully so that the communication efforts are clear, consistent, and understood. Consistency and impact are the keys to communicating messages effectively. The critical issue for those responsible for communicating information throughout the organization is how to improve the accuracy, flow, and acceptance of relevant messages so as to reduce uncertainty about what is happening to its lowest possible level. A simple acronym may aid in identifying four key elements in this process: ACTS (see Fig. 7.2).

A = attitudes

C = content

T = techniques

S = situation

FIGURE 7.2   Communication ACTS

Attitudes consist of the beliefs, feelings, and predisposition toward behaving that people consider about the people, objects, and events with which they come in contact. All three features of attitude function together so as to reinforce each other. Thus, if we believe you are an honest person, we feel positively toward you, and then we are predisposed to accept an invitation from you to watch a live soccer match. However, if we believe that you are dishonest, we'll probably feel negatively toward you, and then we will be inclined not to accept what you have to say. Thus, when we get an e-mail message from you, we may be suspicious of it and have a tendency to automatically question and even reject what you have to suggest.

Individuals have attitudes toward people with whom they associate on the job. They have attitudes toward the kinds of work assignments that they are given. They have attitudes toward the ways in which people instruct and inform them, and they have attitudes toward where they work and how they are to get things done. Attitudes may be the most critical of the four aspects of communication. Attitudes are usually more important in affecting what we understand and what we do than are the content, techniques, and situations of communication. If you seem to be having a problem, the first place to look is in the attitudes of those with whom you are trying to communicate.

Content has to do with the topics and ideas encompassed by the messages being distributed. The content of a message may be a policy, a practice, or an action. The content may be identified by the answer to the question "What is this message about?" However, this is a question not only of content but also of intent. Is this message a veiled attempt to talk about efficiency on the job when it appears to be about rewards? Employees may be suspicious of messages when they have negative attitudes and thus misinterpret what the sender of a message actually intends; on the other hand, a critical and suspicious employee may in fact unveil a devious intent on your part, if you are not perfectly honest with all employees.

Techniques have to do with the ways in which messages are distributed to organization members. Information about techniques has a long history and a strong foundation in both research and practice. However, there are costs and benefits to be balanced whenever communication techniques are considered. As a rule, the more personal a technique is, the more costly it is to use; thus, getting information out to a thousand employees in face-to-face conversations is more costly than sending everyone a printed questionnaire. The more sensitive the content of a message is, however, the more effective it is when personal techniques are used; thus, if you need to correct an employee, a face-to-face meeting is usually the most effective technique.

Six requirements govern decisions in the use of communication techniques: availability, relevance, impact, response, skills, and cost. *Availability* means that a technique can be used only if it is available in the organization. After an inventory of available techniques, you can decide whether to add other ways to make a more effective communication program.

Relevance means that a particular technique is appropriate for the specific kind of message being distributed. If the purpose is to inform organization members about the results of a marketing campaign, a memo might be most relevant. If the information contains complex details that need to be reviewed regularly, a written technical report may be more relevant.

Impact means that the technique chosen creates the appropriate impression on those who get the information. Thus, often a glossy, colorful brochure may be used even though a more routinely printed piece might handle the information adequately, because a little flair may have more impact.

Response means that different techniques are used depending on whether an immediate or a delayed response from those getting the information is deemed desirable. Thus, if you don't need to have an immediate response from employees, a memo may do; but if you want to see how individuals are reacting as soon as possible, you may want to call a meeting.

Skills mean that the technique chosen must fit the sender's abilities to actually prepare the message and the receiver's abilities to comprehend it. A glossy brochure should be used only if you have someone capable of producing such a piece. If employees' education levels are limited, complex manuals of instructions may not be appropriate.

Cost means that the amount to be invested fits into the budget. The technique that is considered the least costly tends to be selected for routine messages, but for high-status people and nonroutine information, more costly techniques are often used.

Situations mean that messages received and the conditions under which they are received have an effect on how they are interpreted. Communication is a social process, making the very nature and structure of an organization a powerful influence on how messages are understood.

Status relationships are powerful influences on the meaning of messages. For example, a colonel may speak sharply to an Army recruit without repercussions, but as a member of the local Chamber of Commerce, the colonel may appear out of place speaking sharply to another member of the chamber. The circumstances and the locale always have an effect on messages.

Recognition

Recognition is a powerful way to establish a presence. There are several ways to recognize people that go beyond the classroom. If you think about them broadly, you might see the importance of both formal and informal recognition events. Informal events include spontaneous recognition for things in the learning environment. This includes visits to markets where you "catch" people doing things right. Plan to have several giveaways that you can carry easily. Pins, bookmarks, caps, pens, and thank-you cards all make good giveaways that reinforce appropriate behavior and results and allow the name and identity of the function to spread throughout the various businesses and markets you visit. Recognition, in effect, reinforces the communication strategies of the T&D function. It is important to brand giveaways, as well as materials, products, and services. This also adds to the visibility of the training and development function.

Another way to recognize both people and organizational accomplishments is to provide training and development awards. Choose the market with the best score on the T&D review document, discussed in Chapter 6, to present with the award. Possible options include giving awards to categories of winners, such as gold, silver, or bronze awards for superior scores, outstanding scores, and excellent scores. Involve senior management in presenting the awards to raise their awareness of your products and services and the process that exists in maintaining a quality system. This approach will go a long way toward establishing credibility. Also consider other awards, such as most supportive market business unit, best training and development manager of the year, and most helpful subject matter expert in the design of sessions. One of the main reasons for an extensive recognition program is to involve members of the organization so they can aid you in achieving the goals of the T&D function.

CAPABILITY: INDIVIDUAL, FUNCTIONAL, ORGANIZATIONAL

Individual

The primary purpose of the training and development function is to increase the capability of individuals, functions, and the system as a whole. It may seem obvious, but all organizations are composed of people, and people have different capabilities. The entire T&D system, from headquarters to markets to customers, has been given the opportunity to close the gap between what business units have and what they would like in terms of employees' abilities. To realize this opportunity, the T&D function must identify and define how it is going to build individual capability.

The needs assessment in each of the regions, countries, and markets may have uncovered some general discrepancies, but the assessment process must become very specific to obtain individual information. Individual T&D plans may contain adequate detail for discovering some development needs. However, if they don't, take a level or layer within the local markets and gather information from individuals to build a picture of training and development needs within each area and, hence, within the organization as a whole.

You might start by setting up individual interviews with members of a target group to find out to what extent the T&D function could help them resolve problems. If you bring a common need to the surface, arrange for specific training and development in that area of capability. Many T&D people assist in doing needs analyses without realizing it is part of a larger strategy. Even if it seems unlikely that you can arrange to have individual meetings with members of the target group, you might work on raising an awareness of potential training and development opportunities among business unit managers. Be sure to include the development of capabilities of training managers whose interests might trickle down to individuals.

Functional

The next level involves investigating whether the markets have provided any products and services that encourage their employees to grow in their technical capabilities. A discussion with functional leaders and managers about the competencies and capabilities required of a particular function is a good place to start. Out of the discussions, create a draft "road map" that you can float among heads of other similar functions in other locations to obtain their input. Again, the idea is to build a complete curriculum by function and decide whether you can design and offer products and services or whether you will need to purchase skills development products from others. Where possible, decide how you can use the Internet to assist in training and development, especially if you are just providing functional information rather than a full development program. Having products and services available to categories of employees begins to standardize the ways in which things are done in a particular function across the world.

Organizational

What are you doing to increase the capability of the total organization? Has a specific goal or target been set that requires a broad organizational development strategy? Is there information that has to be disseminated quickly, or is there information about cultural shifts or new initiatives that need to be consistently understood? For example, the introduction of a new quality program would be an initiative that might involve an extensive information dissemination effort. Another initiative might be a new customer service emphasis to counter the negative effects of a product recall. A cultural initiative might call for an entire market to be exposed to and assimilated into a global community. Although these may be large and probably complex problems to solve, the key to success is realizing that the bigger the problem, the greater your impact— *if* you solve the problem.

RESPECT: INTEGRITY, RELIABILITY, AND RESULTS

Ultimately you should focus on winning the respect of all managers and employees in the area, which stems from integrity, reliability, and results. Respect is achieved through integrity, doing what is right for the company and speaking up when there are tough issues; reliability is doing what you say you will do on a consistent basis; excellent results should flow from integrity and reliability. Getting the results that were agreed to allows the T&D function to get more of what it needs the next time. In most organizations, you earn credibility by involving employees, developing capabilities, and acquiring their respect. Doing these activities well and consistently is the formula for success. Ultimately, the way you succeed in an organization is to earn the respect of colleagues and clients. When you produce results and act with integrity and consistency, you will earn the admiration of members of the organization.

Here are some questions to assist you in determining whether you are on the right track: Have all key constituents been included in the planning process? How many different communication channels are being used? How is recognition being used to better the image of the training and development function? How is the capability of individuals, functions, and the organization being developed? Is the training and development function doing what it says it will do? Do the training and development staff act with integrity at all times? Are the training and development staff achieving or exceeding the results that others expect?

PERFORMANCE VERSUS POWER AND POLITICS

Many books have been written about power and politics, and even though these topics are important elements in the success of a T&D function, they are often misunderstood. We cannot stress too much that anyone working at the headquarters level may be faced with office politics and power struggles. Nevertheless, successful T&D functions must focus on getting the job done, so that performance is enhanced, and not getting caught up in politics. The goal is to improve human performance in delivering the company's products or services, rather than to figure out how to manage corporate politics.

This discussion is not about power, because T&D functions rarely have much positional power, although they can have a positive influence in organizations. At the same time, this discussion is not about whom has more staff or a larger empire, since empire building lasts only until the next cutback. So if you're trying to build an empire, do it because you are satisfying the needs of the people and the organization. If you are building for the sake of having a grand structure, you will lose the game very quickly.

As the head of the T&D function at an intermediate level—the division or region—your most important goal is to guide the function through the hills and valleys of organizational politics so the staff can do their work with the many business units they assist. Increasing the capability of every one of the training professionals who work in the organization should be foremost in the minds of your staff. Local staff members reflect the corporate T&D function and you as its leader. If local staff do not have the capability today, headquarters must help build them for the future.

A TRUE STORY

A colleague on a rotational project assignment who was working in our corporate headquarters asked, "Why aren't we following the traditional design process?" The answer was, "Let's try to explain with an analogy. The traditional design process works well when people have a common base of knowledge and experience around training and understand what the process can do for them. Imagine that the idea of common knowledge is the ground floor of a building. You must understand that we have people here who are still in basement 3; we have others who have not even reached the building, and still others who are stuck in traffic." You shouldn't get caught up in trainer's lingo and techniques and lose sight of your goals. Some functional staff may try to lose you with their own technical jargon, and that may be acceptable to them, but it's the job of the T&D function to make sense out of the communication deficiencies of every employee. It takes time to educate a particular client base, and different people are at different stages of understanding what they need from you, why they need it, and how to express what they need from you to resolve a performance problem.

With systems, processes, and infrastructures in place, the element that puts all this at risk is your inability to cooperate and inspire your customer base and solve real problems in the organization. This might be rudimentary, but the higher up you go, the more important understanding people's needs become. A T&D leader has a serious choice to make: How much time are you going to spend building bridges versus the amount of time you spend doing the actual work of running the function? You can get swamped by trying to maintain all necessary relationships, but without quality relationships, administering the details of the function may achieve very little.

So as you think about how to manage relationships, rather than details, you must also think about a few other things before you jump into any business situation. Here are some basic questions that must be addressed as you begin the process of managing a multiple-location T&D system, especially if the headquarters is located thousands of miles away. These questions operate at several levels: corporate, region, division, country, market, local units, and individuals. *Country* encompasses all of the businesses in one nation or national boundary within a region. *Market* refers to a specific business that operates in the country. The term *local units* refers to one of the separate business units or outlets in a market, country, and division or region. The term *individuals* makes reference to one person in a local business unit. Some regions have one business per country, which implies that you should start your questions at the market level. If the company has more than one business unit in a country, then you start at the country level.

The key questions to ask yourself prior to a meeting with a manager in a particular market or local business unit are designed to elicit information that is useful in building a sustainable system. What is the biggest problem in this country today? How about tomorrow and in the future? What is the biggest problem in this market today? How about tomorrow and in the future? What is the biggest problem in the local business unit today? How about tomorrow and in the future? What is the biggest problem being faced by individual employees today? How about tomorrow and in the future?

These four questions aid the T&D function in discovering where potential problems exist. However, the most important question to ask is this: "How can we help?" Sometimes you obtain clues rather than answers to key questions. If you do get definite answers, then you are halfway there in terms of your ability to provide assistance. In most cases, however, when you ask difficult questions, individuals may not be able to answer them very directly or completely. That is, they may know many answers in terms of today, and they may be able to speculate about tomorrow's problems, but it is unlikely they will be able to project far into the future. Nevertheless, answers to even some of the questions may assist you in devising plans to solve some problems, which may now just be a beginning.

Avoid the "training and development for its own sake" syndrome. You can easily get caught up in numbers and train everyone with little regard to purpose or direction. To have a significant impact on any region, country, market, or individual, you must find performance issues at each of those levels and then respond to them. The given is that this problem can be solved with a T&D solution. If a complete solution isn't possible, there may be pieces of information, tools, and practices that you can make available to local managers that will aid them in working through their difficulties. Sometimes, lending your expertise to facilitate a business meeting or to identify someone who can help may be all that is necessary. At other times, you may be able to do more by offering a quick team-building activity to put some spark into a meeting.

CRITICAL QUESTIONS TO ASK DURING INTERVIEWS WITH BUSINESS MANAGERS

To manage a multiple-location T&D function successfully, you must constantly keep abreast of what is going on in the organization and anticipate solutions before they are needed. One way to anticipate solutions is to think through a number of issues before you meet with a client. For example, ask yourself anticipatory questions such as these:

- What new initiatives are going to be launched at the corporate, regional, or market levels?
- What potential technological changes might have an impact on this business?
- What significant leadership or managerial changes might occur, and what impact will they have on support for current and future projects?
- What has the T&D function done for markets and business units lately, from which it can get support to move projects ahead?

Once you meet with the client, consider how you can assist them in terms of new corporate, regional, or local initiatives. For instance, at the corporate level, T&D may prepare constituents for the train-the-trainer's rollout. At the regional level, T&D may help conduct an important event or provide advance notice when corporate is ready to launch a corporate-sponsored event. At the local level, T&D may be able to assist headquarters in preparing materials for the big event. Continue with each key question and formulate a strategy.

One of the worst things you can say when interacting with managers is, "Let me find out about that." When local unit managers ask a question such as, "Steve, have you considered new ways of doing product training over the Internet?" The response "Let me find out about that" might not appear bad on the surface, but deep down it shows you have not been thinking about or anticipating solutions to that issue. In reality, you should be minimally thinking about issues that have a one- to two-year lead time. The ideal response would be to say, "You know, Bill, I have been thinking about that, and here are several options." How will you recognize when you have reached this kind of holistic thinking? The answer is simple: when solutions you suggest are needed or sought by senior management. You will be very close when you can talk about various possible approaches when questions come up. And you will be ready when you feel that you are ahead of the game.

HOW TO DEVELOP SPARE CAPACITY

As your performance grows and you deliver excellent results, people tend to expect your output to grow at the same rate (see Fig. 7.3, line B). However, expectations rise faster than output since people tend to expect more when you deliver (Fig. 7.3, line C); therefore, you have to raise your capability considerably higher to satisfy the new demand (Fig 7.3, line A). This is important if you want to stay ahead. Such demands, however, require spare capacity.

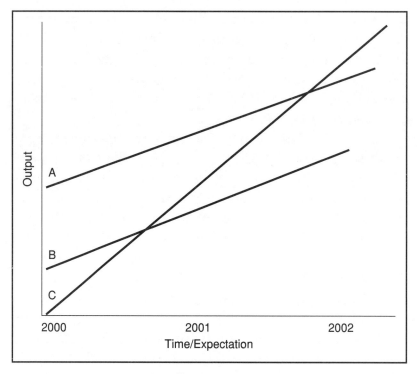

FIGURE 7.3 Time and Expectations

Look at the time and expectations chart in Figure 7.3. The
x-axis represents the volume of your products and services; the y-axis represents the time and expectation line.
Simply put, the chart shows that people's expectations
tend to run ahead of a person's capacity to deliver. So how
do you handle these expectations?

To maintain a sustainable multiple-location T&D system, you need to be able to contend with additional
demands in which everyone seems to want something
now or last week. How do you get those additional projects completed? Do you add more staff, increase the budget, find more external resources, or work longer hours? An
unusual phenomenon happens when you start to deliver
on your promises. The word gets around and everyone
wants to jump on the bandwagon. The reason is that they

realize you can actually help them, that you can do the very thing they want, and that they either lack the time, resources, or knowledge to do what they want. In many cases, a strong T&D function becomes a call to action for many people. Nobody wants to be left behind, and they suddenly have a "problem." Granted, it is a good problem; however, if the problem is not managed, your working life can become too complicated. You may find that you are not delivering on those additional requests, and your credibility begins to drop. This is tough, because it takes significantly more effort to rebuild credibility than it takes to create it the first time around. This overload usually happens in the second and third years when the function's track record speaks for itself. By then, most people have seen or experienced the work of the function, and it has been showing results. People like it when things go well. You will too, if you plan to be in a leadership position.

One of the things a good T&D professional should do is always plan to deliver more than is expected by having the "spare capacity" to do it or by knowing how it can be done through other means. Some ways to develop this spare capacity is to avoid putting all things down on your yearly plans. Leave some open spaces that can be used for additional requests. Another way is to make sure you have access to external vendors or other internal resources to do the job, preferably in several countries or locations. Locate suppliers who are trying to break into the business and will "bend over backward" for you to obtain your business.

Discuss the overload issue, in monthly or quarterly review sessions, with your team to help members anticipate upcoming bottlenecks. For example, Steve was once in charge of all international training at a headquarters. His team consisted of administrative support and himself. He decided to hold a department meeting. Six people attended the meeting: the administrative support, two contractors, an ex-contractor visiting from out of town, and one person on a rotational assignment. It appeared that he had a huge department.

The key to spare capacity is to budget for it and include these extra people in the planning process so they can provide ideas and insights as part of the planning process. Being a part of planning, they understand more of the total picture, making it possible for them to pick up the slack when they are needed. Taking the time to think about what you might say in such a meeting will help to clarify your own thinking. Here are some ways that you can develop your own spare capacity:

1. Make sure that projects have multiple beneficiaries, either now or in the future. That is, do a project that is urgent for someone else, knowing that the results, with some modification, could help several other markets.

2. Identify external vendors who can pick up the slack.

3. Use "working at the headquarters" as a developmental assignment for promising internal staff.

4. Find out who has done this kind of work before in your internal training network.

5. Get members assigned to the project from the sponsoring market.

6. Work with individuals in various markets on mutually beneficial projects.

7. Budget for spare capacity.

HOW TO RESPOND TO REQUESTS FROM MULTIPLE LOCATIONS

A reason for unexpected overloads is simultaneous requests from different locations or constituents. When such requests come into the regional or divisional office, the manager and staff have some difficult decisions to make. They have to decide which tasks should be accepted or rejected, which requests should be done first, which alternatives should be recommended, and which ideas should be ignored. Once you decide what to do, some conflicts might develop around which project should be done first. Here we establish criteria to help you select the projects to do first. The correct choices should enhance your credibility, flexibility, and survivability in the organization.

First, select projects that will benefit someone now or in the future. Before you solve a market, a functional, or an individual problem, ask yourself, "Who will benefit?" If you solve a market problem, the question is "Does the solution satisfy the GM, the CEO, or someone else? Does the CEO even know about your efforts, or do you know whether it is even important to the CEO? The same questions need to be asked for both the functional and the individual levels. The credibility of the T&D function depends on how well you make choices in response to these questions. So think about all the projects and activities you are working on and identify who will benefit from each one and why each project is important to someone.

When you are faced with projects that seem somewhat equal in importance, which ones do you do first? Which requests do you give in to and accept? Which ones do you defer to someone else? Which ones do you ignore? You only have twenty-four hours in a day, which is not sufficient to meet all of the pressing needs of every potential client. So how do you prioritize your limited time and resources? The answer lies in knowing what completing the project buys in return and how people who really matter view that project. Your ability to get the right projects done on time might gain you some credibility. The key is to assess the situation, use your organizational knowledge, and make the right call. As you already know, just because some think the project will solve one of the organization's biggest problems does not mean that the project has to be done first. For example, timing may be of greater concern. Is this the right time to do this particular task? In addition, agreeing to do a project may have more to do with how much personal time and effort the project will require than either importance or timing; that is, can you find someone on your staff to do the work, or can you delegate it to an outside resource? You also need to consider the person for whom you are doing this project and what impact that person has on the T&D function. If you have ways of getting two or three tasks completed at the same time, then all three clients may see their particular project as the most important one. Let people know that you are working on several projects, so the completion of their specific task tends to appear all the more significant.

If you correctly answer the question "Which project should we do first?" you are going to be thought of as flexible. Contacts will say, "The training and development function made an effort to reprioritize its busy schedule for my request. They must be good guys; after all, I am one of the most important functions in the company since they bent over backward to help me." Everyone thinks that they are the most important. Your ability to do extra projects is due to your "spare capacity." The ability to have spare capacity becomes very important in completing projects that can provide some leverage later. So when you respond, "OK, I'll move the schedule ahead a week for you," you know you have the capacity to do it.

Which requests do you ignore? Sometimes you have to watch for those who make urgent requests. They don't really need them completed until tomorrow but claim they need them yesterday. Your ability to find out what the real needs are and what is going to change allows you to ignore some things with no consequence, because the scenario will have changed anyway and your efforts would have gone to waste. Responding professionally while postponing things that might change allows you to give a reasonable answer, while ignoring the smokescreen of "I needed it yesterday."

Some decisions require a consulting mind-set rather than a trainer mind-set. The difference has to do with the frame of reference you have as you approach your internal clients. External consultants want to be your business partner, performing as one who understands your business issues, to be a value-added information source All of these goals apply to you as an internal consultant. Even though you do not consult with outside companies, your training and development role definitely allows you to engage in consulting activities in your own company or market. For example, to be a consultant, you need to understand the business and provide tools, processes, and solutions to problems. Even from a pure training design role, you should have the same mind-set as a consultant. You have to determine whether the problem requires a training solution and, if so, how you should approach the design project. Remember that your clients may be in "basement 3" in terms of your expertise. Most of your customers are not T&D professionals like you. All you have to do is help them complete the job they want done in the time frame they want; however, you know where to make decisions that abbreviate the process, allowing you to finish projects on time or even ahead of schedule. There is a definite choice about how programs should be put together, and that is a choice you have to make. We use this three-month, three-week, three-day, three-hour framework as a guide to thinking about design. As you know, development time is specific to each project.

Three-month design—Use the full three-month design when you have a large project that may have an impact on a large number of people in the company; you need to go through the full design process of needs assessment, task analysis, design document development, pilot, and summative evaluation.

Three-week design—Use a three-week design when a needs assessment is not required, where the content is well defined, and where a work need is done primarily on structuring and sequencing content. The first course may also serve as a pilot, or you may want to do a trial pilot with developers and subject matter experts rather than with an independent sample of subjects.

Three-day design—When the content has already been identified, use the three-day design. Focus on preparing the training manual and session procedures. Concentrate on the process of information distribution and effective learning and on what the participants should be able to do when they complete the session.

Three-hour design—When a manager walks into your office and says that he or she has to have a three-hour workshop this afternoon, which was originally agreed to be a half-hour presentation, what do you do? Focus on the techniques for getting involvement and group interaction and on your facilitation methods. Sketch out a two-hour outline, with key questions to ask, and group discussion activities to conduct.

In all of these scenarios, you actually use the same skills, although you compress them for different amounts of preparation time. The process may not be as pretty in the shorter times, but it should be about as effective. There may be skeptics of fast design. However, if your GM came and asked you how long it would take to develop a training program to fix a predetermined business problem, and you gave him a choice of three months or three weeks, which do you think he would choose?

Now, if you gave him a choice of three weeks or three days, which would he choose? You can see that we are not advocating sloppy design. What we are suggesting is that you should have ways of designing training sessions more quickly if the situation demands it. We're not sure that everyone has the ability to be that flexible. However, with things changing as fast as they are in business today, survival may depend on your ability to make adaptations. You should at least be thinking about how to compress design time.

INTERNET OPTIONS

In the arena of more efficient training administration, spare capacity, and compressed design time, the Internet really gives the T&D function a new dimension. Registration from anywhere in the world is almost routine; getting automatic registration confirmation and program reminders is expected. Payment is done through e-commerce systems, and follow-up to the learning event is done on a regular basis. The thread that runs through all this is that electronics is now doing a lot of the routine.

You can even print and distribute training materials close to or at the site of the training session, especially if you're training at an international location and not in a position to spend extra money for overnight air packages. In fact, there are companies who manage the whole logistics of printing, packaging, and delivering for you, over the Internet, with distribution centers around the world.

CONCLUSION

Many training and development managers make the mistake of focusing on the work, technical skills, and the materials development and assume that getting the task done right is all that matters. But you know that building the right relationships is just as important as being competent. Competency in the field is a given. Getting your work done through others is the acid test for surviving, especially in an arena where your success depends on others. In the case of a T&D manager, those significant others would include subject matter experts, participants, human resources personnel, and business unit managers. Regardless, political skill is the oil that makes the model work within the organization, minimizing friction. It is the variable that allows the department to live and breathe rather than stagnate under the weight of too much competence and not enough organizational support. Your ability to survive and thrive during the installation of a new system may require enhancing your own social and emotional intelligence.

CHAPTER 8

HOW TO BUILD ORGANIZATIONAL CAPABILITY

People are the common denominator of progress. So . . . no improvement is possible with unimproved people, and advance is certain when people are liberated and educated.

JOHN KENNETH GALBRAITH

The same concept that has successfully launched the regional center can now be applied to the entire organization at the corporate level. In this chapter we will defend the role of the T&D function in enhancing total organizational capability and how to build individual, functional, and cross-functional capability using specific tools. And will all that development lead to change? Inevitably. So, we will speak to the matter of change management also.

The T&D function provides a range of activities that add value to and strengthen the overall capability of the organization. Products and services develop the performance of individuals, facilitate team development, and improve the way the organization as a whole achieves its goals. The business need and ability of local and regional teams often determine which products and services can actually be delivered. The caveat to this is that senior managers may need to be educated about the breadth of activities that the T&D function can undertake.

The activities that the T&D function should deliver to enhance the overall capability of the entire organization can be arranged according to four capability buckets: (1) building individual capability, (2) building functional capability, (3) building process capability, and (4) building external capability. To perform the tasks associated with each capability, the T&D function must possess the ability to carry out the traditional tasks, including consulting and change management, to assist in developing the organization's total (four buckets) capability.

Why is this necessary? Whatever T&D does, it must improve performance. Performance improvement may need to occur at individual, operational, organizational, and external organizational levels. This includes all of the elements that are part of the value chain of the organization, including suppliers, vendors, partners, franchisees, and customers. If we assume that T&D teams perform only the traditional roles of training and development by preparing training sessions to address skills and knowledge gaps for individuals and teams, then the function will miss the opportunity to help build total organizational capability. This insight is very important to well-run organizations. The ability to provide a wide variety of services truly transforms their role and scope into that of a performance improvement group. To have the most impact, the various training and development teams must be able to do not only traditional training everyday jobs—analysis, design, development, implementation, and evaluation—but also performance and process improvement, workplace learning, and consulting. However, having the desire and fulfilling the need are two different things. We will attempt, in this chapter, to provide suggestions concerning how to achieve "total organizational capability."

WHY SHOULD THE T&D FUNCTION ENHANCE TOTAL ORGANIZATIONAL CAPABILITY?

Why should the responsibility for creating total organizational improvement be part of the vision? Third parties often facilitate change management and process improvement interventions more effectively than individuals in operational units. A person or team that does not belong to the business unit receiving the service is often able to approach problems more realistically. Training professionals not only possess the essential skills, but they are also located where they have an objective view of the unit under analysis. This is why organizations often use external consulting firms, the ultimate third party, if they themselves do not posses the internal capability. Where a regional center exists, staff there may take this neutral role.

Another advantage of using internal consulting resources is, in the longer term, the decision to use outside consultants is always one of cost, continuity, competence, capability, and having the flexibility of "resident" internal units. However, if cost, competence, and internal staff cannot satisfy flexibility concerns, then external consultants might very well provide a valuable service to the company.

Training and development teams should, whenever possible, step up and take on this wider-ranging consulting role. It is in the best position within the organization, from a neutrality and capability standpoint, to provide appropriate consulting services. When you couple that capability with knowledge of the business and an understanding of the organization's internal nuances, it is an unbeatable combination. If the organization wants to have a body of internal consultants at its disposal, we suggest that a plan to develop those skills in the local training teams be developed as soon as possible, if they are not currently present in the regional training team.

The change from a traditional role to a broader "consulting role" can be achieved through a well-devised game plan. This means that the organization must carefully define the end results, develop the processes, and use the appropriate tools for building total organizational capability. Also, the T&D function must adopt new change management practices that help the broader objectives and goals "stick" in the organization.

HOW TO DEVELOP ORGANIZATIONAL CAPABILITY

Developing organizational capability has three key stages: (1) define the end result, (2) develop processes, and (3) use appropriate tools. The tools and processes are designed to build six areas of capability: individual, functional, cross-functional, cross-organizational, external, and change management and capability-sustaining systems. Let us review each of these categories and what is involved in them.

Define the End Result

To start the process, knowing what is to be achieved is important. To do this, get together with a senior sponsor or executive team and help them describe the preferred end results that would increase their business's capability. They should answer questions such as these: What will things look like, what processes should be in place, and how might people participate more in the business process in the future? Although there are many ways to specify end results, choose a method that has been used by the company or business unit in the past, especially if it is already part of the company's strategic planning process.

Develop Processes

As you know, unless visions, action plans, and projects become codified into everyday processes, the likelihood of them being successful is very low. For their success to be ensured, the organization needs to identify all key processes, the steps involved, their exact sequences, and who specifically performs each step, including the time frame in which they happen.

The tool called "process mapping" (Rummler & Brache, 1990) provides a systematic way of obtaining, documenting, and capturing information to develop all categories of organizational capabilities. Process mapping identifies how information flows within the organization and how you can use that information to improve the process. Mapping helps determine how changes can be made in the organization so that more efficient and robust processes are built. To encourage this type of initiative, the unit's senior management should identify one key process and have the T&D team use it as a test to see whether the process is functioning well in the organization and then demonstrate how mapping can help improve the process.

Such a test enables the organization to understand the resources required and the amount of time and effort also required. If you get beyond the test, be certain to have either a function or person accountable for making the process of mapping happen. Also remember to make the project a priority for senior leadership and provide regular updates on progress; otherwise, the whole project might fail.

Use Appropriate Tools

Based on senior team input, the T&D team should determine the resources required to achieve the desired end. Ask the senior team to describe in detail what it sees as the requirements and changes needed to make the end result

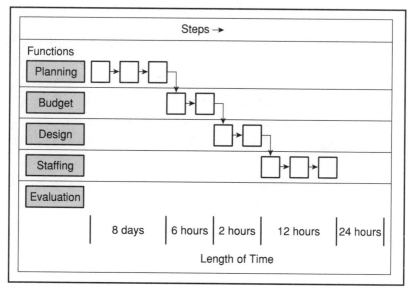

FIGURE 8.1   Process Flowchart

happen. To document this clearly, produce a detailed process flowchart of how the plan might unfold in the organization (see Fig. 8.1).

All training personnel, especially a regional team (when present), should be trained in process-mapping skills. Again, several good resources for this are available, including the foundational book, *Improving Performance,* by Rummler and Brache. Even if process-mapping skills are not used as prescribed, the knowledge of the methodology is essential for effective consulting and may be used at other times. Let us now look at the requirements for each of the capability categories.

Building Individual Capability

An individual needs assessment could ascertain what constitutes appropriate competencies (skills, knowledge, and decisions) for employees in various locations, then interventions could be devised that build those skills in individuals. The interventions are usually reflected in the T&D services and sessions. Quite often, it is possible to design development activities for specific positions in the markets. Figure 8.2 illustrates some managerial competencies.

One of the most visible ways to build competence is to broadly advertise its package of standardized courses by publishing a catalog or creating visibility through other appropriate company literature.

Building a series of courses that focus on positions involves treating supervisors, first-time managers, upper

	Unskilled
Hiring and Staffing	• Doesn't have a good track record in hiring and/or staffing • May clone him- or herself or focus on one or two preferred characteristics • May look narrowly for people who are similar to him or her • May play it safe with selections • Doesn't select much diversity • May not know what competence looks like, lack criteria, or assume he or she just knows • May lack the patience to wait for a better candidate
	Skilled
	• Has a nose for talent • Hires the best people available from inside or outside • Is not afraid of selecting strong people • Assembles talented staff

FIGURE 8.2 Managerial Competencies

managers, directors, general managers, and vice presidents as categories of employees as job levels within the company. The sessions are usually developed around skills for job progression. In marketing, for example, the position might be new hire, marketing assistant, and through to marketing vice president. An alternative to designing courses for positions is to create classes for each of the specialized functions in a business. In marketing, the courses might include advertising, promotions, and consumer research.

The business functions approach assumes that personnel in different business functions must have special skills to perform their jobs but also need some increased competence in managerial skills such as critical thinking and organizing. This approach is common and involves hiring experts in specific functions to provide training for each specialty.

In many cases, soft skills such as leadership, problem solving, and decision making are relevant for many positions and specialties in the company for which general skill development is appropriate. The medium of delivery may use face-to-face sessions or computer- or Web-based training (WBT) to supplement existing modes of delivery.

One way to encourage individual capability development is to provide certificates, bachelor's degrees, or advanced degree programs for the staff. Organizations usually collaborate with higher-learning institutions to provide this type of instruction. In some cases, the curriculum is especially tailored to suite the organization. However, the organization usually participates in the institution's current programs and enjoys the benefits of having content that has been taught to other students. One other consideration, when dealing with company-sponsored higher education, is whether you should have all the students in one class from one location, country, or region or whether you should have a mix of students participating from different parts of the organization and from different geographic areas. This choice is really an issue of scale—or how many potential employees the company can release for development sessions. Different companies have used both methods, but something more positive comes from having a mixture of students who bring diverse thinking, backgrounds, and networking opportunities from many industries and companies in the same session. For example, the University of Adelaide in Australia offers one of its courses to employees from Singapore and other Asian countries. The course, leading to an MBA, is offered as a summer course in Adelaide but is offered in January to employees of Asian companies during their winter season.

Building Functional Capability

One way to develop functional skills is to create a capability system for individual business units. The T&D team helps each unit define, review, and measure the performance of individuals in each operational area. This assists each function in defining the capabilities needed within its own operational area.

A functional capability system is developed by constructing a model of the main activities and roles within a function, then developing a series of questions that inquire into and review that model, checking to determine whether employees are following the requirements. Finally, the progress of individual employees is measured against the functional standards. Figure 8.3 shows a functional model for human resources to illustrate the kinds of activities identified.

Ultimately, this process should be developed for each functional area within the organization, such as marketing, finance, operations, facilities, franchise support, human resources, and research and development. Each function should develop its own assessment using a model, questionnaires, and other measures to determine its functional capability or end state.

Strategic HR Management	Change Agent
• Strategy integration	• Change leadership
• Cost management	• Change management
• Strategic processes	• Functional leadership
• Strategic staffing	
• Benchmarking	

HR Basics	Employee Champion
• Administrative effectiveness	• Internal equity
• Staffing process execution	• Culture enhancement
• Compensation and benefits	• Knowledge management
• HR information systems	• Reward and recognition
• HR policies	
• Performance management	
• Regulatory compliance	
• Turnover and retention	
• Training and development	
• Labor and employee relations	
• Health and safety management	

FIGURE 8.3   Functional Model for HR (Adapted from Robert Ulrich)

Having the model in place allows functions to define their work through questions and have measures in place to track progress. While developing these models, ensure that the skills have been validated through the functional heads at headquarters. This is important for the credibility of the output, which speaks to the validity of the process. The corporate T&D function may also use these models to disseminate the review process throughout all of the business units under its review. The instrument shown in

Chapter 6 is a good example of how a model is built for a particular function.

The models and questionnaires give the headquarters or regional T&D function a mechanism by which to evaluate the capabilities of each business unit, by assessing each of its functions using the measurement system and review process for continuous improvement. If the functional training and development approach is implemented, it can also be used to narrow the gaps between desired capability and current performance. This then becomes a complete functional capability system.

WHY DO YOU NEED A MODEL FOR EACH FUNCTION?

It's amazing that few people in any given function understand the scope of the entire function. For many, the model of performance in the function is the first document in which someone has articulated the requirements of their specific function. If managers use the questionnaire to assess their understanding of the function, then the model becomes their first scorecard. Table 8.1 portrays a functional scorecard. Again, possessing minimum criteria against which to measure work performance may be the first experience that employees have had with a standard measure. If used in an ongoing fashion, the model may be used to track improvements in the capability of the function over time. Tricon Restaurants International has successfully deployed such a system, called BMU Self-Sufficiency, to all their major markets around the world. Pat Murtha, senior vice president, human resources, leads this effort and says, "BMU Self-Sufficiency is possibly our best answer to measuring functional gaps across our system and using that knowledge to ensure that we reach our business goals."

TABLE 8.1 Baseline Assessment for Human Resource

HR Basics	1	2	3	4
Administrative effectiveness			X	
Staffing process execution			0	X
Compensation and Benefits			X	
Turnover and retention		0		X
Training		0	X	
HRIS			X	
HR policies	0		X	
Regulatory compliance			X	
Performance management		0	X	
Labor and employee relations			X	0
OH and safety management				
Employee Champion				
Internal equity		0	X	
Culture management			0	X
Communications		0	X	
Reward and recognition			X	
Strategic HR Management				
Strategy integration	0		X	
Cost management			X	
Strategic processes		0	X	
Strategic staffing		0	X	
Benchmarking	0		X	
Change Agent				
Change leadership		0	X	
Change management			X	
Functional leadership			0	X

Legend:
1 = Does not meet standard
2 = Generally meets the standard but needs improvement
3 = Meets the standard
4 = Best in class

Another use of this function's capability system is as an excellent coaching and support tool for T&D staff in supporting various markets or business units. The model allows headquarters, divisional, and regional teams to focus on areas that require assistance and support, rather than simply making quick market visits in which market and business units put their best foot forward. The T&D function can focus on true capability building.

Models and questionnaires are useful ways to orient new employees by focusing on what is important to their role. Imagine this: You have a new college hire who wants to know what is required of her in the new marketing job. You give her a model that defines all of the key areas that are important. Under each of the categories is a series of questions that probe the extent to which the new hire knows the processes and procedures for the marketing function. Where the assessment indicates she has knowledge gaps, the new marketing employee is able to identify the places where she might find information or where she might attend a training session to get the information. In fact, now that the employee has the questions, she may even simply ask others in the department for answers. Additionally, personnel from many functions may gain greater familiarity with other functions through the medium of the model and its associated questions, so that they can be better prepared to participate in a rotation.

HOW WOULD YOU USE THE PROCESS FOR YOUR T&D TEAMS?

Now we'll focus on the training and development function itself. Most professionals concede that headquarters, divisional, and regional T&D staff should engage in and develop their consulting skills on a regular basis. For example, they should use a consulting approach when reviewing a unit's T&D function. The approach to reviewing and auditing the T&D function described in Chapter 6 provides a consistent set of criteria and measures to use in aligning training and development activities in each market. The review also identifies opportunities, called *coaching moments* or *consulting moments*, for headquarters or regional staff to assist the local market training and development team members to close gaps that are identified. The experience of the local T&D teams at other levels in the organization comes together to build total organizational capability. In fact, headquarters and regional staff might find working comfortably with local T&D teams is the best way to distribute best practices from market to market.

Most important is the quality of the in-depth time that headquarters or regional staff spend with the leaders of functions during the review process. If nothing else, the local managers appreciate having a model and an objective rating system against that they can be judged by or for use as a self-development tool.

The review exercise uncovers gaps in the capabilities of individuals in various markets that T&D staff can help address, either as a group or on an individual basis. Sometimes the gaps can be matched with products and services offered routinely by the training and development function, especially if the services and sessions are designed to improve operational capability. Using these opportunities as often as possible, the headquarters and regional T&D functions have the ability to assess, educate, and reward teams over multiple locations.

BUILDING CROSS-FUNCTIONAL CAPABILITY

From a training standpoint, the keys to building cross-functional capability are twofold. You must provide cross-functional training and development opportunities, and you must create cross-functional opportunities by ensuring that your products and services are made available to the entire organization. This availability encourages employees to engage in development activities from other functional areas as part of their individual development plans. Compliance and participation can be monitored during yearly performance appraisals. Employees in one function should get exposed to the mechanisms of another function so they can better appreciate the true nature of the work involved. This type of insight is invaluable, especially for more senior leaders and those who work in matrix organizations or on cross-functional process teams.

Sometimes companies offer orientation sessions that cover the entire breadth of the business, touching on key aspects of each facet. These overview sessions are usually mandatory for certain levels of staff so everyone understands how each function fits into the core processes of the organization. These programs also focus very heavily on shared metrics and cultural issues relevant to the organization's locale.

Organizations that focus on processes versus solely technical tasks are on the right path in terms of building true organizational capability. Process capability emphasizes cross-functional teams and core processes to improve the way in which work is performed. Beyond that, there is the use of reward and recognition practices to reinforce the teams that work across functions to solve organizational problems.

CROSS-ORGANIZATIONAL CAPABILITY

How does the organization ensure that all business units and operations on any particular distribution line have all the same process, tools, and measurement systems? How does one make sure that the best practices from one business unit are made available to the others? The best way is to have someone oversee a best-practices program so it is integrated into yearly performance objectives. This is why, earlier in this chapter, we suggested that the headquarters team, or even a regional T&D team, was in the best position to sponsor this type of program.

Best practices need to be identified and disbursed throughout the company by means of forums, regional meetings, newsletters, management reports, and central best-practice databases. The particular methods and how they are used may be a matter of local preference, but dissemination is achieved most effectively by choosing one or more methods and getting everyone accustomed to using them. To further enhance the exchange of best practices, create a way of rewarding business units for adopting ideas to improve performance.

BUILDING EXTERNAL (SUPPLIER, CUSTOMER, FRANCHISEE) CAPABILITY

To many organizations, their external partners, whether suppliers, customers, or franchisees, are really an extension of the company. With that philosophy, the external partners have the right to be part of the development opportunities provided for internal employees. The caveats here involve what programs are made available to external partners and the extent to which they are offered without charge.

What should be made available? This question is really answered by asking the reverse question: How open is the organization to external clients in terms of using company T&D products and services? A corollary question concerns how much support the organization is willing to provide to external partners. The level of support can be thought of in terms of the same categories discussed earlier; that is, individual, functional, and cross-functional activities and products and services for franchisees and other clients and partners. Let's look at the issues involved in providing a T&D function for external partners.

One major question needs to be answered: Can external clients have access to all of the management, leadership, operations, technical, and other training and development products and services offered by the T&D function? A positive answer may be obvious at first, but consider that some topics may be appropriate only for internal staff. Some products may contain content with legal, license, or contractual information.

In terms of training and development for some skills in specific functions, external organizations might not need the information and skills to perform their work. However, in many organizations, it would be a waste of resources if the best practices and assessments were not shared for the common good of the entire system. If this is the philosophy, then all tools and functional assessments should be made available. The only issue concerns the case of suppliers or customers who may share the same relationship with your competitors. Does this mean that you are increasing the potential of proprietary tools being shared with your competition?

If you can't trust your current partners, you should not be doing business with them. However, there are ways of numbering or copyrighting information that you think is critical to protect it. Otherwise, it may be "better to be occasionally cheated than to be perpetually suspicious" (B. C. Forbes).

At its heart, the issue may be one of having enough experienced staff members and other resources to support such activities. Will management complain about the attention and resources being given to people outside the company? If you're making money, the question may become "How do you 'turn off' the revenue tap once you realize that it is a great source of income?"

Another issue concerns whether external organizations should have access to your consulting services. Do you want to make any of your consulting services, such as process mapping, troubleshooting, process improvement, and quality systems implementation, available to others? If you do not have the resources to handle external demands, it is better to have a series of approved vendors that can be recommended to provide these services than trying to offer them yourself.

The other way to handle this is to provide train-the-trainer sessions to develop consulting skills within the partner organizations. Thus, limited resources can be maximized and used in quality control or other support functions, as opposed to actually doing the work.

CAPABILITY SUSTAINING SYSTEMS: CHANGE MANAGEMENT

Helping partnering organizations sustain their capability draws heavily on change management. If this is a company-wide initiative, to be rolled out to all business units, a timetable and a train-the-trainer schedule should be created to cascade the know-how from headquarters to regions to individual business units. The T&D function can assist with follow-up and team meetings to move the change process ahead. If change is an initiative started in one of the business units within a region, then the regional T&D function should make best practices from other business units available to everyone. Eventually, a few best practices should be selected for institutionalization and featured by all units in the company. If you want to be more formal, you might set up a review committee to ensure that the practices selected are indeed best practices.

SUSTAINING PERFORMANCE WITH REWARDS

Instead of detracting from performance improvement, contests and competitions significantly aid in building a culture of support. Recognition is an excellent way to encourage sustained performance in organizations. For example, in Asia a certificate or "piece of paper" that says you have attended and completed a course or series of sessions is paramount. This means that in Asia, you must create pieces of paper to meet that requirement. Some companies go as far as to award joint diplomas with universities or have industry approval and certification for qualified in-company courses and certificate programs. Others have created certificates to which stars or medallions can be attached to denote that additional sessions have been completed. Others give pictures framed with written comments from the other participants. Others have report cards that tell what has been completed and what is left to take. Many companies give pins, and staff wears them with pride. Although these are simple ideas, they can go a long way toward motivating staff. However, if you want longer-term results, you must integrate all T&D products and services into building blocks that are tied to feedback and performance appraisals and annual individual development plans that complete a full-performance management cycle.

CONCLUSION

The success of a T&D function may somewhat depend on the extent to which it can contribute to the total organizational effort by building the organization's capability to meet its goals and achieve its objectives. In fact, total organizational capability may be at the heart of an effective multiple-location T&D function.

Multiple-location training and development requires more than just a program or two and some training activities. Concern about the entire organization and the various methods that training and development can be delivered and distributed to locations far distant from headquarters may require thinking about the whole system and how newer electronic and other technological systems allow employees to take more control over their own development.

A CALL TO ACTION

When you come to a fork in the road, take it.

YOGI BERRA

We live in a time of global economics and global expansion. The most significant trend within this global economy is regionalization. A company can hardly do business in new markets without considering the problems associated with managing across multiple locations and training and developing employees in the variegated national venues of the world. This global expansion has increased the complexity of the corporate system and the complexity of managing it and requires corporations to examine how they manage multiple-location operations. This unparalleled opportunity is tempered only by the risk inherent in failing to manage the people and processes needed to fully utilize that opportunity.

For the training and development function, the risk lies in failing to reach the mission-critical goals of managing knowledge in multiple locations, supporting diverse cultures, and enhancing performance across geographic and national boundaries. But the very nature of a multiple-location system embodies paradoxes that challenge even the best management talent. Are we seen as business managers or learning specialists? Do we position ourselves closer to the people or closer to the power? How do we attain the most effective balance between control and autonomy? What will your decision be? For some, the answer lies in adherence to a system encompassing all aspects of the training and development process. We believe that the more "systemic" the function, the more credibility and impact it has. Toward that goal, the traditional training model, ADDIE, can be applied in a larger way to create and manage a multiple-location system.

The more diverse and geographically dispersed the organization is, the more important it is to have a well-defined and carefully managed system. A multiple-location T&D system can be characterized as a set of building blocks with each block representing an element, from analysis to evaluation. The system can be viewed from two major perspectives—the training and development perspective and the business perspective. From either perspective, the steps are identical: analysis, design, development, implementation, and evaluation. The steps thus represented can be used to develop high-level organizations and structures using the very same systematic process thinking for which it was created in the design of simple training sessions. But this system and all systems require business processes and expert management to support them. Which systems model is appropriate for your organization?

The traditional business processes play two roles. Traditional business paradigm wraps itself around the system to define the external environment while the specific functions of the paradigm enable the system to operate. They support the system in the external environment by being the common denominator that links the system to all other functions within the organization. Internally, they become tools of the trade when adopted by training and development and used as any business unit would use them. As a separate organization within the total system, training and development must incorporate the major business functions—marketing, operations, finance, human resources, and management information systems—and use them in fulfillment of its function.

One nontraditional tool that T&D must adopt is that of technology. In the same way that classic business processes enable traditional training functions to operate, so technology empowers the multiple-location system to operate by enabling communication, standardization of processes, and evaluation procedures. Since T&D is responsible for sharing best practices and implementing on-line learning, it has an obvious role to play in the selection of technology and in clarifying issues around technology implementations. Technology is needed to unify the training hierarchy, from unit to corporate levels. In addition, technology is increasingly used by T&D functions as a training tool, expanding media choices beyond the traditional classroom and video. Thus, technology supports various aspects of the T&D operation, as seen in the multiple-location system model, but differs in its application to each block of the model. How will technology play a role in our organization, now and in the future?

The management of regional operations is unique in the world of training. Whether operating as a cost center or a revenue center, in a new facility or a virtual environment, with a large staff or small, unique issues affect the operational performance of the region. Relationships with corporate will vary based on the amount of control vs. autonomy assigned to the region. A director supervises staff that is probably responsible for design, production, and delivery of regionwide programs in support of corporate efforts to establish consistent process, uphold standards, and build company culture. In addition, the region may have its own goals such as providing consulting and change management expertise for the business units across the entire region. From reporting relationships through structure and staffing, the design/organizational structure phase of the model addresses these pertinent issues.

Regions follow corporate mandates and standards but exercise more control over regional and local unit functions, especially at the operations level. Relationships with other regions may best be described as strategic alliances where each regional office is part of a loosely coupled system in which they support each other in a collegial way. The internal structure of a regional function is no less unique. While size and internal structure drive staffing, the key to success lies in following a model for selecting and preparing the staff. The larger decision regarding whether to build a freestanding regional facility brings together both internal and external considerations involving funding of the center, pricing, and revenue streams. Whether housed in a freestanding facility or operating as a virtual center with limited staff, the regional center becomes a center of information and activity uniting the various arms of the multiple-location system. Are regional structures right for your organization?

A multiple-location training system cannot survive without regular reviews and the use of assessment tools in the regions. Thus, the system review document (Fig. 6.1) sits at the heart of establishing and maintaining a high-performance T&D function. The review measures performance against a baseline, assesses compliance with the system, motivates employees, and rewards accomplishment. In a multiple-locations system there is simply no other way to accomplish all this in a cost- and time-effective way. Growth and development can only occur when managers and employees know what is expected, have the tools necessary to meet those expectations, and are motivated by the promise of rewards. The beauty of the process and tool described involves primary stakeholders and uses their natural talents, allowing them the opportunity to develop without overt criticism. Few evaluation systems achieve their goals in a fashion that enhances the self-respect and confidence of employees. This audit process makes a review supportive of self-respect and enhances the confidence of employees. Using the review at corporate level may be helpful in establishing support and acceptance for a gap analysis approach in that it sends the message that all levels of the organization are engaged in self-analysis toward improvement. The regional director's role, then, would be to employ a teaching/consulting approach in developing local units and assuring compliance with the model. How will you assess your system?

Once the multiple-location system and system review document are developed and operational, attention must turn to ensuring that all locations know how to operate skillfully within their political environment, for the implementation of a system is not dependent on competence alone. The very best training and development plans amount to little unless each field location is able to build bridges to critical power centers at all levels of the organization. Nine critical success factors can be identified that cover the gamut from planning to attitude to reliability. These success factors are important because many training and development managers focus technical skills or program/materials development and assume that getting the task done right is all that matters. But getting your work done through others is the acid test for surviving, especially in an arena where your success depends on the acceptance of others. In the case of a T&D manager, those significant others would include subject matter experts, participants, human resources personnel, and business unit managers. Political skill is the oil that makes the model work within the organization, minimizing friction. It is the variable that allows the department to live and breathe rather than stagnate under the weight of too much competence and not enough organizational support. How do you ensure that your ML managers have these skills?

The same concept that has successfully launched the regional center can also be applied to the entire organization at the corporate level, for the T&D function has a valid role to play in enhancing total organizational capability. The T&D function provides a range of activities that add value to and strengthen individual ability, functional capability, cross-functional capability, and cross-organizational capability.

In the field of human resource development, regional (multiple-location) training and development systems are relatively new, but they play a crucial role in the natural extension from global companies to global training. With the advent of new electronic technology, information can be distributed to multiple locations at breakneck speeds, often with the danger of overloading those local units. The regional system is able to step in, facilitate the creation of knowledge out of the information, make it compatible with local circumstances, monitor the effectiveness of the distribution system, cultivate the corporate culture so the essential messages are sent, and enhance both individual and organizational capability.

At the same time, a regional training and development function can minimize distances and effect critical standards of excellence by using electronic technologies, being sensitive to local customs and being close to the people in those locations. With regional staff members who can translate instructions and directives, personal contact ensures greater accuracy and consistency. At the same time, personal contact allows coaching and mentoring to occur with increased productivity and satisfaction among market employees. Establishing a regional training and development center and coordinating system is a bold move, but an essential one. We encourage you to take the "fork in the road" and build a multiple-location system that works in your organization.

COMMUNICATION
CLIMATE INVENTORY

Please respond to *all questions* as honestly and frankly as you possibly can.

In *no way* will your identity be associated with your responses nor will your responses be used in such a manner as to jeopardize you or your job.

Unless the wording of a particular item specifically indicates otherwise, respond in terms of your own impressions of the entire organization in which you work.

Indicate your response to each item by *circling just one of the five numbers* in the right-hand column. PLEASE DO NOT OMIT ANY ITEM! Use the following code to interpret the meaning of the numerical symbols:

5 = Circle this number if, in your honest judgment, the item is a true description of conditions in the organization.

4 = Circle if the item is more true than false as a description of conditions in the organization.

3 = Circle if the item is about half true and half false as a description of conditions in the organization.

2 = Circle if the item is more false than true as a description of conditions in the organization.

1 = Circle if the item is a false description of conditions in the organization.

PLEASE, DO NOT ATTEMPT AN INTENSIVE "WORD ANALYSIS" OF THE QUESTIONS. AND—OF COURSE— YOUR RESPONSES SHOULD REFLECT YOUR OWN JUDGMENTS, NOT THOSE OF OTHER PEOPLE. THERE ARE NO RIGHT OR WRONG ANSWERS.

Answer all questions in terms of your impressions concerning your own organization!

You may now go to the next page and begin.

1. Personnel at all levels in the organization demonstrate a commitment to high performance goals (high productivity, high quality, low cost).

   5 4 3 2 1 (1)

2. Superiors seem to have a great deal of confidence and trust in their subordinates.

   5 4 3 2 1 (2)

3. Personnel at all levels in the organization are communicated to and consulted with concerning organizational policy relevant to their positions.

   5 4 3 2 1 (3)

4. Subordinates seem to have a great deal of confidence and trust in their superiors.

   5 4 3 2 1 (4)

5. Information received from subordinates is perceived by superiors as important enough to be acted upon until demonstrated otherwise.

   5 4 3 2 1 (5)

6. All personnel receive information that enhances their abilities to coordinate their work with that of other personnel or departments and that deals broadly with the company, its organization, leaders, and plans.

   5 4 3 2 1 (6)

7. A general atmosphere of candor and frankness seems to pervade relationships between personnel through all levels of the organization.

   5 4 3 2 1 (7)

8. Avenues of communication are
available for all personnel to
consult with management levels
above their own in decision-making
and goal-setting processes.

$\quad$ 5 4 3 2 1 (8)

9. All personnel are able to say
"what's on their minds" regardless
of whether they are talking to
subordinates or superiors.

$\quad$ 5 4 3 2 1 (9)

10. Except for necessary security
information, all personnel have
relatively easy access to information that relates directly to their
immediate jobs

$\quad$ 5 4 3 2 1 (10)

11. A high concern for the well-being
of all personnel is as important to
management as high performance
goals.

$\quad$ 5 4 3 2 1 (11)

12. Superiors at all levels in the organization listen continuously and with
open minds to suggestions or reports
of problems made by personnel at all
subordinate levels in the organization.

$\quad$ 5 4 3 2 1 (12)

**Thank you very much for taking
the time to complete this inventory!**

REFERENCES

Abrams, Rhonda. 1999. "Don't Judge a Book by Its Cover: The Kinko's Story." *Business Week* (12 February). Available: www.businessweek.com/smallbiz/news/coladvice/book/bk9 90212.htm (6 July 2000).

"Asymetrix Learning Systems Announces Availability of Ingenium 4.0." 2000. Available: www.asymetrix.com/pr/ ingenium40.html (10 July).

Barron, Tom. 1999. "The Fruits of Joint Labor in Boeing's QTTP Website." *Technical Training* (September–October).

"The Boeing Company Saves $9 Million, Trains 21,000 Managers." 2000. Available: www.digxpr.com/boeingapp.html (20 June).

"Boeing Deploys Progressive Networks' RealVideo Streaming Media Technology on Its Massive Intranet." 1997. *Intranet Design Magazine* (8 May). Available: idm.internet.com/news/ blurb47.html.

"Boeing Takes Care of Business at a Glance." 1999. *Corporate University Collaborative* (July–August). Available: www.traininguniversity.com/magazine/jul_aug99/cover3.html (19 June 2000).

Bolman, Lee G., and Terrence E. Deal. 1991. *Reframing Organizations: Artistry, Choice, and Leadership.* San Francisco: Jossey-Bass.

Brethower, D. M., and K. A. Smalley. 1998. *Performance-Based Instruction: Linking Training to Business Results.* San Francisco: Jossey-Bass.

Briody, Dan. 1999. "Dow Turns to the Web to Drive Down Training Costs." *InfoWorld* (20 September): 48.

"BT and Futuremedia Win First Solstra Contract from Ford Motor Company." 1998. Available: www.futuremedia.co.uk \ (4 September 1998).

Careless, James. 1998. "Pumping Up Sales." *Satellite Today* (July). Available: www.satellitetoday.com/viaonline/backissues/1998/0798sales.html (23 June 2000).

Chaudron, David. 1998. "Global Training Gets High-Tech at Buckman Labs." *HR Focus* (April): S12.

Cherry, Colin. 1957. *On Human Communication: A Review, a Survey, and a Criticism.* New York: Wiley.

Ciancarelli, Agatha. 1998. "Purchasing Goes to School on Company Intranets." *Purchasing* (18 June): S25–S26.

Davis, J. R., and A. B. Davis. 1998. *Effective Training Strategies: A Comprehensive Guide to Maximizing Learning in Organizations.* San Francisco: Berrett-Koehler.

"Digital Xpress Signs Arthur Andersen as First Customer." 1996. Boeing Web site, 24 September. Available: www.boeing.com/news/releases/1996/news.release.960924a.html (6 July 2000).

Dobbs, Kevin. 2000. "Who's in Charge of E-Learning?" *Training* (June): 55–58.

Duff, Kerry. 2000. "New Kinko's Center Offers State-of-the-Art Training." *Business Journal* (January): 35.

"Filling the Dealer Training Pipeline at Ford." 1997. *Training* (October): A26–A28.

"First in Flight: The Boeing Company Cuts Training Administration Time, Money, and Waste with Syscom Inc.'s TrainingServer Family of Management Software." 1998. *TrainingServer.com.* Available: www.trainingserver.com/CaseStudy/indexBoeing.html (3 July 2000).

Fister, Sarah. 2000. "Reinventing Training at Rockwell Collins." *Training* (April): 64–70.

Flynn, Gillian. 1997. "Bank of Montreal Invests in Its Workers." *Workforce* (December): 30–34.

"Ford Motor Company [U.S.] Buys into Solstra for Further Three Years." 2000. Available: biz.yahoo.com\prnews\00629\Ford_design.htm (29 June 2000).

Fusillo, Gloria. 1999. "A Taxing Enterprise." *AV Video Multimedia Producer* (May): 29–30.

Fryer, Bronwyn. 1998. "MCI Goes Live." *Inside Technology Training* (October): 18.

Gagne, R. M., and K. L. Medsker. 1996. *The Conditions of Learning: Training Applications.* Orlando, FL: Harcourt Brace.

Girard, Kim. 1998. "Ford Drives Workers to Web for Training." *CNET News.com* (December). Available: news.cnet.com/news/ 0-1007-200-336274.html (20 June 2000).

Greenberg, Richard. 1998. "Corporate U. Takes the Job Training Field." *Techniques* (October): 36–39.

Greengard, Samuel. 1998. "'Virtual' Training Becomes Reality." *Industry Week* (19 January): 72.

Greengard, Samuel. 2000. "Keyboard Courses at Work or Home." *Workforce* (March): 88+.

"GTE Selects Asymetrix Learning Systems to Create Internet Based Training Solution for 25000 Employees." 1999. click2learn.com Web site, 4 January. Available: www.asymetrix.com/pr/gte.html (12 July 2000).

Hanner, Mark. 1999. "Intranet University: Chemical Company Saves Millions with Web-Based Training." *Communication News* (July): 12.

Herling, Richard W., and Joanne Provo, eds. 2000. *Strategic Perspectives on Knowledge, Competence, and Expertise.* San Francisco: Berrett-Koehler.

"Internet Co-Worker Training Improves Customer Support." 1999. LeadingWay Web site. Available: www.leadingway.com/ clients_kin.htm (5 July 2000).

Karon, Roy L. 2000. "Bank Solves Compliance Training Challenger with Internet."

E-Learning Magazine (March). Available: www.elearningmag.com/ articles/march00/banksolved.htm (3 July 2000).

Kelley, R. E. 1985. *The Gold Collar Worker.* Reading, MA: Addison-Wesley.

"Kinko's Chooses Livelink to Manage Knowledge Enterprise-Wide." 1999. Kinko's Web site, 14 June. Available: www.kinkos.com/about/pressrel_18.html.

Kiser, Kim. 1999a. "E-Learning Takes Off at United Airlines." *Training* (December): 66–70.

Kiser, Kim. 1999b. "Instructional Designer." *Training* (August): 31.

Klatte, Arline. 1999. "A Degree in Hamburgerology." *CBS Marketwatch* (6 October). Available: aolpf.marketwatch.com/ source/blq/aolpf/archive/19991006/news/current/hamburger.asp (26 June 2000).

Krebs, Michelle. 1999. "LM Dealers to Get LS Training." *Automotive News* (15 February): 48.

"LearnLinc 4.0 Raises the Bar." 1999. Available: www.dtac.com\ company\news001.htm (3 August 1999).

Limerick, David, and Bert Cunnington. 1993. *Managing the New Organization*. Chatswood, Australia: Business and Professional Publishing.

Lohmann, Janice Snow. 1998. "Classrooms without Walls: Three Companies That Took the Plunge." *Training and Development* (September): 38.

Marquardt, Michael J., ed. 1999. *Developing Human Resources in the Global Economy: Advances in Developing Human Resources*. San Francisco: Berrett-Koehler.

Martinez, Anne. 1998. "HP Reaches Out—140,000 Employees Tune In." *Inside Technology Training* (June): 42.

Mateyaschuk, Jennifer. 1999. "LearnLinc 4.0 Allows for Larger Classes." *Information Week Online* (2 August 1999). Available: www.informationweekonline.com\746\inc.htm.

"Melanie Brisbane: A QTTP Success Story." 2000. IAM-Boeing Joint Programs (May–June). Available: www.iamboeing.com/ jointprograms/news/2000/2000_may_jun/may_jun_2000.htm (23 June 2000).

Mintzberg, Henry. 1993. *Structure in Fives: Designing Effective Organizations*. Englewood Cliffs, NJ: Prentice Hall.

"Motorola University Implements Plateau Enterprise Learning Management System." 2000. Plateau Systems Web site, 18 January. Available: www.plateausystems.com/news.html (10 July 2000).

"Motorola University's Learning Forum." 1999. *Corporate Universities International* (January–February): 9.

Nye, Joseph S., ed. 1968. *International Regionalism: Readings, Part II*. Boston: Little, Brown.

Odenwald, Sylvia B. 1993. *Global Training: How to Design a Program for the Multinational Corporation*. Homewood, IL: Business One Irwin.

Pace, R. Wayne, and Don F. Faules. 1989. *Organizational Communication*. Englewood Cliffs, NJ: Prentice Hall.

Pemberton, Jeff, and Thomas Pack. 1999. "The Cutting-Edge Library at Hewlett-Packard: Bringing Together Knowledge, Access, and Tools." *Online* (September–October): 30–34.

Rayl, Karen. 1998. "GTE's Training Goes High-Tech." *Workforce* (April): 36–40.

Rucker, Rochelle. 1999. "Maintaining Market Leadership through Learning: How Motorola Uses Technology to Provide the Right Knowledge at the Right Time to Its Globally Dispersed Personnel." *Supervision* (September): 3–6.

Rummler, G. A., and A. P. Brache. 1990. *Improving Performance: How to Manage the White Space on the Organization Chart.* San Francisco: Jossey-Bass.

Rummler, G. A., and A. P. Brache. 1995. *Improving Performance: How to Manage the White Space on the Organization Chart* (2nd ed.). San Francisco: Jossey-Bass.

Sabia, Carol, and Connie Cassarino. 1999. "Learning Online— Best of All Worlds." *Inside Technology Training* (October): 44.

Schaff, Dick. 1999. "Where ERP Leads, Training Follows." *Training* (May): ET14–ET16.

Schein, Edgar. 1990. "Organizational Culture." *American Psychologist* 45: 109–119.

Smith, Denis, and Mary Conyngham. 2000. "Restructuring the Arthur Andersen Information Service." Ninth Australasian Information Online and On Disc Conference and Exhibition. Available: www.csu.edu.au/special/online99/proceedings99/201c.html (6 July 2000).

Solomon, Charlene Marmer. 1999. "Continual Learning: Racing Just to Keep Up." *Workforce* (April): 66–68.

Stoerp, Mary. 2000. "Getting Trained in Your Own ILEC's Backyard: MCI WorldCom Provides Fiber Optic Cable Restoration Course at Its CEU." *Outside Plant Magazine* (February). Available: www.ospmag.com/features/2000/getting_trained_in_your_own_ilecs_backyard.html (July 2000).

Swanson, R. A. 1996. *Training for Performance System: Field Handbook.* St. Paul, MN: Swanson and Associates.

Swanson, R. A., and E. F. Holton. 1999. *Results: How to Assess Performance, Learning, and Perceptions in Organizations.* San Francisco: Berrett-Koehler.

Swanson, R. A., and E. F. Holton. 2001. *Foundations of Human Resource Development.* San Francisco: Berrett-Koehler.

VanAdelesberg, D., and E. A. Trolley. 1999. *Running Training Like a Business: Delivering Unmistakable Value.* San Francisco: Berrett-Koehler.

Walton, J. 1999. *Strategic Human Resource Development.* London: Financial Times.

Whaley, Tammy, and David Wright. 1999. "Methodology for Cost-Benefit Analysis of Web-Based Telelearning: Case Study of the Bell Online Learning Institute." *American Journal of Distance Education* 13: 24–44.

Wilkins, Alan L. 1983. "Organizational Stories as Symbols that Control the Organization." In L. Pondy and others (eds.), *Organizational Symbolism.* Greenwich, CT: JAI.

Wilkins, Alan L. 1984. "The Creation of Company Cultures: The Role of Stories and Human Resource Systems." *Human Resource Management* 23, no. 1: 41–60.

Wilkins, Alan L. 1989. *Developing Corporate Character: How to Successfully Change an Organization without Destroying It.* San Francisco: Jossey-Bass.

Williams, Frederick, and Herbert S. Dordick. 1983. *The Executive's Guide to Information Technology.* New York: Wiley.

INDEX

Action plan, after performance
    evaluation, 158–160
Activity base, 133
ADDIE model, 14–15
    activities related to, 15
    analysis/business input stage
        (phase 1), 20–34
    business performance objec-
        tives, 27–29
    business perspective in, 18–20
    curriculum planning, 42, 43
    delivery of training, 46
    design/organizational structure
        phase (phase 2), 34–40
    development/products and ser-
        vices phase (phase 3), 40–46
    electronic training, 42, 44
    environmental scan, 21–27
    evaluation system, 39–40, 55
    evaluation/system output phase
        (phase 5), 55
    human resource requirements,
        29–31
    implementation/execution
        stage (phase 4), 47–55
    infrastructure building, 38–39
    instructors, 51
    learning environment in, 47, 49,
        50
    learning process, 51–55
    materials, 45–46
    objectives, 37–38
    and size of center, 112, 113
    and staff selection, 119
    steps in, 18
    subject matter experts (SMEs),
        44–45
    target group competence re-
        quirements, 31–34
    target group competency pro-
        files, 31
    vision and values, 34–37
Analysis, design, development, im-
    plementation, evaluation. See
    ADDIE model
Analysis/business input stage
    (phase 1), ADDIE model, 20–34
Arthur Andersen Consulting
    Company, technology-based
    training, 100–101
Arthur Andersen Virtual Learning
    Network (AAVLN), 101
Attitudes
    and communication, 169
    meaning of, 169
Audit. See Performance assess-
    ment
Awards, 172–173
    benefits of, 72–73
    Training and Development
        Award, 156, 159

Bank of Montreal, technology-
    based training, 103–104
BASELINE, 98
Best practices, in training, 123,
    156, 161
BMU Self-Sufficiency system,
    201
Boeing Aircraft Company,
    technology-based training,
    89, 95–96
Branding, of organization, 71–72
Brandon Hall, 89

Buckman Laboratories, technology-based training, 104–105
Budget
  communication as item, 138, 171
  construction of, 63
  departmental, example of, 134
  fixed costs, 132–133
  for language translations, 137
  overhead, 135, 137
  and pricing of services, 139–140
  semifixed costs, 132
  variable costs, 133
  See also Finance
Bulab Learning Center, 104
Business functions
  communication plan, 68–69
  finance, 62–63
  human resources, 63–64
  management information systems (MIS), 65–68
  marketing, 61
  operations, 61–62
Business managers, role of, 10
Business performance objectives, ADDIE model, 27–29
Business processes, traditional, 212–213

Capability of system, 173–175, 181–184
  additional projects/requests, 182–183
  and change management, 208–209
  cross-functional capability, 204–205
  cross-organizational capability, 205–206
  external capability, 206–208
  functional capability, 174, 199–201
  functional scorecard for assessment, 201–203
  of individuals, 173–174, 196–199

organizational capability, 175, 193–196
  and performance improvement, 192
  spare capacity concept, 183–184
  types of capabilities, 192
Career Enhancement University, 98–99
Career Explorer Web, 95–96
Catalog, of programs/activities, 72
Change management, to sustain capability, 208–209
Click2Learn Ingenium, 87
Coaching moments, 204
Code Division Multiple Access (CDMA) technology, 105
College of Learning Technologies (CLT), 92
Communication, 168–172
  about performance assessment, 160
  and attitudes, 169
  as budget item, 138, 171
  and content, 170
  and desired response, 171
  elements of process (ACTS), 168–169
  impact of, 171
  methods of communication, 168, 170
  relevance in, 170–171
  and status relationships, 171–172
Communication climate, 70–73
Communication Climate Inventory (CCI), 70, 217–220
  and cultural sensitivity, 70–72
  elements of positive climate, 70
Communication function, aspects of, 11
Communication outputs
  awards, 72–73
  catalog, 72
  newsletters, 72
  yearly schedule, 72
Communication plan, 68–69
  elements of, 69
  issues addressed by, 68

Condit, Phil, 96
Consulting service, as revenue
  source, 142
Content, and communication, 170
Control function, central versus
  regional control, 11–15
Corporate culture, 7–8
  and communication, 71–72
  meaning of, 7
  strong culture, benefits of, 8
  symbolic aspects, 7–8
Cost center, pricing of services,
  130–131
Cost models
  items for constructing model, 139
  pricing model, 139–140
  regional T&D centers, 138–141
Costs
  Web-based training, 88, 90
  See also Budget
Cross-functional capability, 204–205
Cross-organizational capability,
  205–206
Culture
  corporate culture, 7–8
  cultural sensitivity and local
    employees, 70–72
  and language, 25, 137
  and learning process, 51
  national culture, 6–7
Curriculum planning
  ADDIE model, 42, 43
  curriculum map, 42, 43

Decision-making, participative, 70
Dedication, of new facility, 128
Delivery, training-related, 46
Design documents, uses of, 135
Design/organizational structure
  phase (phase 2), ADDIE model,
  34–40
DeskTV+, 101–102
Development work, as revenue
  source, 142
Development/products and ser-
  vices phase (phase 3), ADDIE
  model, 40–46

Director. *See* Regional director
Disney parks, 7
Distribution system, global,
  2–5
Divisional managers, role of, 62
Dow Chemical Company,
  technology-based training,
  89, 97
DTAR (define, train, assess, and
  reward), 155

Economic conditions, PESTLE
  analysis, 21–22
Education, higher learning and
  employees, 198
Electronic training. *See*
  Technology-based training
Emotional quotient (EQ), regional
  staff, 116
Employee development, types of
  programs, 64
Employees
  gold-collar workers, 110–111
  involvement in planning,
    166–167
  regional centers. *See* Staffing
    regional centers
Engineering/facilities, as business
  function, 60
Environmental conditions,
  PESTLE analysis, 23
Environmental scan
  ADDIE model, 21–27
  market profile, 25–26
  PESTLE analysis, 22–25
  SWOT analysis, 27
Evaluation system
  ADDIE model, 39–40
  evaluation/system output phase
    (phase 5) ADDIE model, 55
  review document for, 40
External capability, 206–208

Facility building, 124–132
  and corporate plans, 127
  dedication/opening of facility,
    128

external issues, 126
internal issues, 125–126
post-building activities,
129–132
pre-building activities, 128–129
size of facility, 127–128
versus facility sharing, 125
Finance
aspects for T&D, 62–63
budget, 63, 132–138
and facility building, 124–132
issues/problems of, 124
meaning of, 124
pricing of services, 130–132
regional T&D centers, 123–124
Fixed costs, budget, 132–133
Ford Motor Company, technology-
based training, 94–95
FORDSTAR, 94
Functional capability, 174,
199–201
development of, 199–201

Gap analysis, 215
General Telephone and Electronics
(GTE), technology-based training, 89, 97–98
Giveaways, as reward, 172, 209
Globalization
and business functions, 57–59
effects on training and development (T&D) community,
ix, 1
multiple-location distribution
system, 2–5
region, meaning of, 4–5
Gold-collar workers, 110–111
Government funding, as revenue
source, 142–143
Grants, as revenue source, 142–143

Handbook, of tools/procedures,
160
Hewlett-Packard (HP), technology-
based training, 101–102
Holistic approach, staffing regional
centers, 117–118

Human resources
ADDIE model, 29–31
aspects for T&D, 63–64
baseline assessment for, 202
employee development, 64
functional model for, 199–200
and regional T&D, 216
special requirements, 63–64
succession plan, 64
and T&D function, 29–30

Implementation/execution stage
(phase 4), ADDIE model, 47–55
Improving Performance (Rummler
and Brache), 196
Individual capability, 173–174,
193–196
development of, 197–199
and higher learning, 198
Information, meaning of, 6
Information collection, 66–68
on corporate level, 67
on local level, 66
on regional level, 67
Information technology (IT)
roles in technology solution, 79
See also Technology
Infrastructure
building and ADDIE model,
38–39
building and business functions,
60
Institute for Learning, 103–104
Instructor guides, as revenue
source, 142
Instructors. *See* Trainers
Integrated Training Information
System (IT IS), 99
International Business Machines
(IBM), technology-based training, 89, 102–103
Internet
performance assessment,
162–163
and regional T&D centers, 144
training potential, 45, 144, 189
See also Web-based training

Interviews, staff candidates, 119–122
Involvement of leaders, 166–173
  and communication, 168–172
  and planning process, 166–167
  recognition of employees, 172–173

Just-in-time lecture (JITL) learning, 93

Kinko's, technology-based training, 100
K'Netix, 105
Knowledge, meaning of, 6
Knowledge Bank, 98
Knowledge management
  aspects of, 5–6, 6
  and corporate culture, 7
  and performance improvement, 8–9
KnowledgeSpace KMS, 101
KPMG, Web-based training, 89

Language
language barrier and training, 25
  translation of materials, 137
Leaders
  relationship-grid, use of, 166, 167
  and success of system, 166–173
LeadingWay, 100
Learning environment
  ADDIE model, 47, 49, 50
  example of, 47, 49
  management checklist for, 49, 50
Learning management systems (LMS), 87, 105
Learning managers, role of, 104
Learning process
  ADDIE model, 51–55
  management checklist, 53
Learning Space, 102
LearnLinc, 99
LearnShare, technology-based training, 92, 93

Legal conditions, PESTLE analysis, 23
Legal factors, information technology issue, 78
Livelink KMS, 100
Location, of T&D function, 10–11
Logo, 71
LOIS, 87

Management
  and regional operations, 213–214
  support for IT, 82–83
Management development staff, regional centers, 116–117
Management information systems (MIS), 65–68
  aspects for T&D, 65–66
  information collection, 66–68
  software for, 65–66
Managers
  business managers, 10
  divisional managers, 62
  market training managers, 108–109
  for on-line training, 104
  regional managers, 62
  relationship managers, 104
  roles of, 62
Manager's Edge, 87
Market profile, 25–26
  affecting factors, 26
Market training managers, 108–109
Marketing
  aspects for T&D, 61
  communication aspect of, 71–72
  four *Ps* of, 61
Masie Newsletter, 89
Materials, ADDIE model, 45–46
MCI WorldCom, technology-based training, 98–100
Meetings, in planning process, 167
Motorola, 14
  technology-based training, 90, 92–93

Multiple-location T&D system
and ADDIE model, 17–55
as business unit, 59–60
levels of, 178–179
Multiple-location T&D system
goals, 5–9
and corporate culture, 7–8
individual performance improvement, 8–9
knowledge management, 5–6
Multiple-location T&D system
management, 9–15
business managers, role of, 10
central versus regional control,
11–15
communication function, 11
T&D location, 10
Multiple-location T&D system
success
anticipating solutions, 180–181
capability of system, 173–175,
181–184
focus on performance, 176–177
involvement of leaders, 166–173
respect of employees, 175–176
and selection of projects,
185–189
Murtha, Pat, 201
MySource, 105

National culture, aspects of, 6–7
Netg, 92
NetMeeting, 102
Newsletters, 72, 160
Nondisclosure agreement, 135, 136

Objectives
ADDIE model, 27–29, 37–38
for business performance, 27–29
formulation of, 37–38
and organizational structure,
37–38
Operations
aspects for T&D, 62
as business function, 60
Organizational capability, 175,
193–196

stages in development of,
194–196
and T&D function, 193–194
Overhead, budget, 135, 137

Pathware, 87
PeopleSoft ERP, 106
PepsiCo, 2
Per-diem charge, 140
Performance assessment
administration of review document, 156–158
communication of results, 160
follow-up to, 158–160
gap analysis approach, 215
Internet, 162–163
introducing review process,
155–156
post-review skills development,
161–162
reasons for, 154–155, 156
rewards for performance, 159
system review document, 40,
147–153
terms used for, 146
Performance improvement
and capability of system, 192
and knowledge distribution, 8–9
Performance objectives, for business, 27–29
PESTLE analysis, 22–25
macro/micro levels, 21
Planning process, 166–167
employee involvement,
166–167
meetings in, 167
regional leader involvement,
166
Plateau, 93
Political climate, PESTLE analysis,
22–24
Pricing model, 139–140
fully funded option, 139
market price, use of, 140
not funded option, 140
partially funded option,
139–140

Pricing of services, 130–132
  center as cost center, 130–131
  mark-up goal, 131
  revenue sources, 142–143
Processes
  development of, 195
  process flowchart, 196
  process maping, 195–196
  traditional business processes,
    212–213
Provant Inc., 33
Purington, Cliff, 103

Qualcomm, technology-based
  training, 105–106
Quality through Training Program
  (QTTP), 95–96

Recognition. *See* Awards; Rewards
Region, meaning of, 4–5
Regional director, role of, 109–110,
  213, 215
Regional managers, role of, 62
Regional T&D centers
  budget, 132–138
  circle cluster structure, 111
  cost models, 138–141
  facilities, 124–132
  finance, 123–124
  internal organization of,
    111–113
  and Internet, 144
  management personnel of,
    108–110
  market versus business unit
    structure, 114
  organizational structure of, 110
  relationship to corporate struc-
    ture, 108–111, 213–214
  revenue sources, 141–143
  size of center, 113–114
  staffing, 114–123
  structure of, 114–118
Relationship-grid, 166, 167
Relationship managers, role of, 104
Relevance, in communication,
  170–171

Reporting, central versus regional
  control, 13–14
Research and development, as
  business function, 60
Respect, elements of, 175–176
Revenue sources, 141–143,
  142–143
  cautions related to, 143
  types of, 142–143
Review and evaluation. *See*
  Performance assessment
Rewards
  events for, 172
  giveaways, 172, 209
  for staff performance, 123
  for sustained performance, 209
  See also Awards
Rockwell Collins, technology-
  based training, 103

Satellite system, training network,
  94, 96, 101
Schedule
  calendar of activities, 72
  project time frames, examples
    of, 187–188
Semifixed costs, 132
Size of center, regional T&D centers, 113–114
Size of facility, determination of,
  127–128
Social conditions, PESTLE analysis, 21
Software, for management information, 65–66
Solstra, 94
Southwest Airlines, learning environment, 47, 49
Staffing regional centers, 114–123
  basic skill requirements, 115
  candidate selection, 119–122
  candidate selection chart, 121
  holistic approach, 117–118
  internal selection, 120
  management development staff,
    116–117
  staff development, 122–123

Staffing regional centers, *continued*
    staff to task match, 118–123
    and structure of center, 114–115
    and succession planning, 115
    technical staff, 115–116
STS International, 33
Subject matter experts (SMEs), role
    of, 44–45, 104
Succession planning, 64
    and staffing regional centers,
    115
Suppliers, sponsorship from, 143
SWOT analysis, 27
System review document, 147–153

Target group
    competence profiles, 31
    competence requirements,
    31–34
Technical staff, regional centers,
    115–116
Technological conditions, PESTLE
    analysis, 23, 24–25
Technology
    business questions related to,
    76
    cautions/issues related to,
    80–83
    examples of use, 75–76
    and global training, 216
    necessity of, 213
    revamping, case example, 81–82
    roles in technology solution, 79
    technology drivers, 77–78
    and training. *See* Technology-
    based training
Technology-based training, 83–106
    ADDIE model, 42, 44
    features of, 44, 87
    implementation checklist,
    84–85
    information sources on, 89
    just-in-time lecture (JITL) learn-
    ing, 93
    learning management systems
    (LMS), 87
    products, 87, 92

training management system
    (TMS), 87
    Web-based learning, 88–89
Technology-based training
    programs
    Arthur Andersen Consulting
    Company, 100–101
    Bank of Montreal, 103–104
    Boeing Aircraft Company,
    95–96
    Buckman Laboratories, 104–105
    Dow Chemical Company, 97
    Ford Motor Company, 94–95
    General Telephone and
    Electronics (GTE), 97–98
    Hewlett-Packard (HP), 101–102
    International Business
    Machines (IBM), 102–103
    Kinko's, 100
    LearnShare, 93
    MCI WorldCom, 98–100
    Motorola, 90, 92
    Qualcomm, 105–106
    Rockwell Collins, 103
    Tool books, 123
    TopClass, 97
Train-the-trainer programs, 46, 51,
    208
    and regional centers, 112, 122
Trainers
    ADDIE model, 51
    contract trainers, 46
    training team, management of,
    51, 52
Training
    and central versus regional con-
    trol, 14–15
    cost of, 45
    post-review skills development,
    161–162
    staff of regional centers,
    122–123
    and technology, 75–76
    technology-based training,
    83–88
    Web-based training, 88–89
    See also ADDIE model

Training & development (T&D)
in domestic setting, 59
globalization effects, ix, 1
See also Multiple-location T&D
system
Training centers, type of, 14
Training and Development Award,
156, 159
Training management system
(TMS), 87
TrainingServer, 96, 99
Tricon Restaurants International,
155, 201

Upward communication, 70

Value statement, ADDIE model,
36–37
Variable costs, budget, 133

Vendors
contracting work from, 135–137
sponsorship from, 143
Virtual Courseware, 99
Virtual reality (VR), training program, 102–103
Virtual University, 98
Vision statement
ADDIE model, 34, 36
and performance evaluation,
157–158

Web-based training, 88–89
cost savings, 88, 89
costs related to, 88, 90
See also Technology-based
training; Technology-based
training programs
Web site, organizational, 71, 72

ABOUT THE AUTHORS

Stephen Krempl is a HRD professional with over 18 years experience in the field. He is currently Vice President— People Capability, for Tricon Restaurants International in Dallas, Texas. He established and runs their corporate university for their international businesses that operate in over 100 countries. As VP of People Capability he is also responsible for managing the company web portal, which serves as its knowledge management, communication and e-learning platform for franchisees, vendors, and employees.

Prior to joining the corporate offices, he was director of regional training and development in Singapore, serving business units in South Asia, China, and the Middle East. His regional training and development team supported the various countries and was involved in implementing the training and development system that he established.

Prior to joining Tricon Restaurants, he worked in Motorola University's regional operations in Asia where he provided support to suppliers, customers, and Motorola business units. This included providing education and consulting services through a team of consultants and customer service staff to support their quality improvement initiatives. Before that Stephen worked as a training consultant with the Singapore Institute of Management.

The author has conducted in-house workshops and talks in and around Asia for numerous multi-national organizations such as General Motors, General Electric, Singapore Telecoms, RJR Reynolds, and Telecom Malaysia. He currently serves as regional director of the Asian Regional Training and Development Organization and he is past president of the Association for Psychological Type in Singapore.

He completed a bachelor's degree in human resource development and accounting at Brigham Young University— Hawaii and post graduate diploma in instructional design from National Productivity Board—Singapore

Dr. R. Wayne Pace is professor emeritus of organizational leadership in the Marriott School of Management, Brigham Young University, Provo, Utah, USA, and adjunct scholar in the Workplace Research, Learning, and Development (WoRLD) Institute of the School of Social and Workplace Development, Southern Cross University, Lismore, NSW, Australia. He is also a visiting professor of management at the University of Adelaide, South Australia. He serves as corporate advisor to QuicKnowledge.com and STS International, companies in the training and development industry.

He is a specialist in human resource development, organizational communication, and individual and organizational change. His current research and writing focuses on factors that affect worker and organizational learning, vitality, and competitiveness. He consults and conducts seminars on how to energize the workforce for improved competitiveness.

Dr. Pace has authored *Organizational Communication* (Prentice Hall, 3rd ed., 1994); *Human Resource Development: The Field* (Prentice Hall, 1991); *The Perfect Leader* (Deseret Book, 1990); *Analysis in Human Resource Training and Organizational Development* (Addison-Wesley, 1989), and thirteen other books and editions, as well as many articles and research reports.

Dr. Pace received his doctoral degree in organizational communication with cognate studies in industrial relations and educational psychology from Purdue University in 1960. He was elected President of the International Communication Association in 1971 and was selected as a Fellow of the American Association for the Advancement of Science in 1971. He was elected President of the Western States Communication Association in 1978, and he was elected Founding President of the Academy of Human Resource Development and selected as Fellow of the AHRD in 1993.

Wayne received the Research Excellence Award from the College of Fine Arts and Communication, Brigham Young University, in 1985, the Outstanding Member Award from the Organizational Communication Division of the International Communication Association in 1986, the Award of Excellence from the Management Development Professional Practice Area of the American Society for Training and Development in 1986, and the Distinguished Scholar Award from the Human Resource Development Professor's Network of the American Society for Training and Development in 1992.

Dr. Pace has been listed in *Who's Who in America* since 1972. He has been on the Board of Directors of local chapters of Rotary and Kiwanis, and he was elected President of the Brigham Young Chapter of the Sons of Utah Pioneers in 1986 and received a Distinguished Service Award after serving as a National Vice President in 1987.

Berrett-Koehler Publishers

BERRETT-KOEHLER is an independent publisher of books, periodicals, and other publications at the leading edge of new thinking and innovative practice on work, business, management, leadership, stewardship, career development, human resources, entrepreneurship, and global sustainability.

Since the company's founding in 1992, we have been committed to supporting the movement toward a more enlightened world of work by publishing books, periodicals, and other publications that help us to integrate our values with our work and work lives, and to create more humane and effective organizations.

We have chosen to focus on the areas of work, business, and organizations, because these are central elements in many people's lives today. Furthermore, the work world is going through tumultuous changes, from the decline of job security to the rise of new structures for organizing people and work. We believe that change is needed at all levels—individual, organizational, community, and global—and our publications address each of these levels.

We seek to create new lenses for understanding organizations, to legitimize topics that people care deeply about but that current business orthodoxy censors or considers secondary to bottom-line concerns, and to uncover new meaning, means, and ends for our work and work lives.

See next pages for other books from Berrett-Koehler Publishers

More books from Berrett-Koehler

Structured On-the-Job Training

Unleashing Employee Expertise in the Workplace

Ronald Jacobs and Michael Jones

Jacobs and Jones describe an approach to on-the-job training that combines the structure of off-site training with the inherent efficiency of training conducted in the actual job setting. *Structured On-the-Job Training* provides step-by-step guidelines for designing and delivering effective training in the actual job setting.

Hardcover, 220 pages, 1/95 • ISBN 1-881052-20-6 CIP
Item # 52206-362 $29.95

Performance Consulting

Moving Beyond Training

Dana Gaines Robinson and James C. Robinson

Performance Consulting provides a conceptual framework and many how-to's for moving from the role of a traditional trainer to that of a performance consultant. Dozens of useful tools, illustrative exercises, and a case study that threads through the book show how the techniques described are applied in an organizational setting.

Paperback, 320 pages, 1/96 • ISBN 1-881052-84-2 CIP
Item # 52842-362 $24.95

Hardcover, 4/95 • ISBN 1-881052-30-3 CIP • Item #52303-362 $34.95

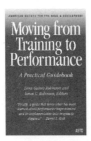

Moving from Training to Performance

A Practical Guidebook

Dana Gaines Robinson and James C. Robinson

Moving from Training to Performance shows how today's performance improvement departments can help organizations meet their service and financial goals. This book offers practical, action-oriented techniques from some of the most highly respected contributors in the field —Geoff Bellman, Geary Rummler, Paul Elliott, Erica Keeps, and others—paired with real-life case studies of organizations such as Johnson & Johnson, Andersen Consulting, Prudential HealthCare System, Steelcase, and PNC Bank, that have achieved exceptional results by making the transition to performance at each level of alignment.

Paperback, 300 pages, 7/98 • ISBN 1-57675-039-6 CIP
Item # 50396-362 $29.95

Berrett-Koehler Publishers PO Box 565, Williston, VT 05495-9900
Call toll-free! **800-929-2929** 7 am-12 midnight

BK Or fax your order to 802-864-7627
For fastest service order online: **www.bkconnection.com**

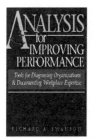

Analysis for Improving Performance

Tools for Diagnosing Organizations and Documenting Workplace Expertise

Richard A. Swanson

Analysis for Improving Performance details the front-end work essential to the success of any performance improvement effort. In clear language and easy-to-follow steps, Swanson shows how to do the rigorous preparatory analysis that defines and shapes successful performance improvement efforts, and maps the critical steps for insuring that a performance improvement program will meet real business needs and objectives.

Paperback, 298 pages, 9/96 • ISBN 1-57675-001-9 CIP
Item # 50019-362 $24.95

Hardcover, 7/94 • ISBN 1-881052-48-6 CIP • Item # 52486-362 $34.95

Human Resource Development Research Handbook

Linking Research and Practice

Richard A. Swanson and Elwood F. Holton III, Editors

Human Resource Development Research Handbook gives practitioners the tools they need to stay on the leading edge of the profession. Each chapter is written in straightforward language by a leading researcher and offers real-world examples to show how research and theory are not just for academics, but are practical tools to solve everyday problems.

Paperback, 225 pages, 3/97 • ISBN 1-881052-68-0 CIP
Item # 52680-362 $24.95

Love 'Em or Lose 'Em

Getting Good People to Stay

Beverly Kaye and Sharon Jordan-Evans

It happens time and time again: the brightest and most talented people leave the company for "better opportunities." Their peers wonder how management could let them go. Managers feel helpless to make them stay. Bigger salaries, loftier titles, and added perks may work for a while, but what employees really want are meaningful work, opportunities for growth, excellent bosses, and a sense of connectedness. Kaye and Jordan-Evans explore the dissatisfactions of today's workers and offer 26 strategies—from A to Z—that managers can use to address their concerns and keep them on the team.

Paperback original, 244 pages • ISBN 1-57675-073-6
Item # 50736-362 $17.95

Berrett-Koehler Publishers PO Box 565, Williston, VT 05495-9900
Call toll-free! **800-929-2929** 7 am-12 midnight

Or fax your order to 802-864-7627
For fastest service order online: **www.bkconnection.com**

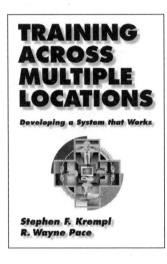